HOW LONG
TO VISITING DAY?

HOW LONG TO VISITING DAY?

Creative Role-Playing for Training Camp Counselors

by John James Hickey
& David Fleischner

illustrated by Yvette Silver

Camp Scatico
New York   MMX

First Edition

ISBN: 1450577814
EAN-13: 9781450577816

Cover Design by (JJH)^2
Printed in the United States of America

*To all the counselors
at Camp Scatico
who helped us develop our role-playing
over the years*

ACKNOWLEDGEMENTS

We would like to thank our family and close friends for their encouragement and support during the preparation of this book. We'd also like to thank the many American and international counselors, who helped by sharing their camp experiences with us. We are especially grateful to Neil Seligman for coming up with the title, Lisa Mastrangelo Mernin for her many years of work helping to plan orientations, and Thomas Stevenson for always being a springboard for ideas.

Contents

Introduction

Read on for a soup-to-nuts guide for using role-playing to create engaging, informative, and inspiring training sessions for counselor staff at children's camps. These sessions will get all of your staff involved—from the 20-year veterans in leadership positions to the 17-year-old first-timers. Offered here are not only 100-plus role-playing scenarios covering a broad range of camp situations, but also a step-by-step process for running the training.

Unlike traditional role-playing, the situations provided here come with two descriptions:

- one for the Camper(s), and
- one for the Counselor.

A volunteer from the audience will play the Counselor role and members of your Leadership Staff will play the Camper role(s). The general audience and the Camper will hear both descriptions from The Moderator running the training, but the Counselor (briefed separately by the Assistant) will only hear his half of the situation.

In almost all challenging situations with campers, counselors do not know everything affecting a camper's thoughts and actions. With dual descriptions, the audience and Campers will have a greater insight into what is happening than the Counselor arriving on the scene to resolve the problem. It makes the role-playing more realistic…. and entertaining.

In our experience, the situations usually take about 10 to 15 minutes each to act out and then debrief. We usually cover six in a 60-90 minute training period. Often, we select topics that we want discussed in staff orientation, but to which we do not have the time to devote an entire session: the moment the campers arrive; homesickness; trying out for teams; auditioning for a show….

Getting Started

STEP ONE
Choosing Your Cast

For your role-playing session you will need:

A Moderator: who preps the audience with both sides of the situation (the Camper's and the Counselor's) and debriefs afterwards.

An Assistant: who preps the person volunteering as the Counselor.

The Campers: members of your Senior or Leadership Staff, who are prepped in advance to know the situation. Their jobs are to make the role-play challenging. In our experience, Leadership Staff make great Campers. They get involved in orientation in a fun way that requires little preparation on their part. It's also a way for new counselors to get to know supervisors. Pick Campers that understand how to work an audience.

The Counselor: the person who is volunteering to counsel the Camper.

STEP TWO
Selecting The Situations

In the pages that follow are more than 100 camp situations. Each situation is categorized according to subject, age, and sex. When putting together the program for your training session, try to cover the full range of camper age groups so at least one situation will pertain to every counselor in the audience.

STEP THREE
Prepping The Campers

In prepping the Campers explain that their role is to challenge the Counselor, but that after a few minutes it is best to give ground and let the situation come to a positive conclusion. The opportunity to debrief each situation (see below) will follow, when the discussion will turn to what the Counselor did well (or didn't do well). If the Camper remains antagonistic right through to the end of the role-play, you run the risk of embarrassing the Counselor who has volunteered to participate. There should be some resistance as the situation unfolds, but the Camper needs to allow some positive movement towards a resolution. The Moderator running the activity can point out during the debriefing that a real camper may not give in so easily, but the goal here is to provide an illustration and create a forum for a discussion on problem-solving.

STEP FOUR
Prepping The Room

We find that a horseshoe set-up of the seating works best, with a clear front stage area. Leave as few rows deep as possible so counselors are close to the action. If the room is rectangular, set the front along a longer side. It may help to place a bench or several chairs in the front for the role-players to move from standing to sitting positions as the situation unfolds.

The Activity

STEP ONE
Selecting Volunteer Counselors

Assuming that you will cover approximately six situations in a 60-90 minute training session, we recommend that the participating counselors represent a cross-section of your staff: male/female; returning and first-time; age of the participant; and the age of the groups to which they are assigned. Part of this will follow naturally from the situations you choose as they are categorized by subject, age, and sex.

At the beginning of the session, set the ground rules for all the counselors about the importance of supporting volunteers. Let the entire staff know how much you appreciate participants for setting the tone for the summer with their can-do attitude during orientation.

You may want to have the volunteers lined up before the session begins, perhaps asking the day before who might be interested. You should prep your veteran counselors beforehand that you expect them to role model the camp culture by raising their hands to volunteer (for this and all orientation sessions), and not pressure younger or first-time counselors to pick up the slack. Having said this, you do want some of the volunteer counselors to be first-timers.

STEP TWO
Running The Situations

1. Create an order for all the situations you want to cover. As Moderator make sure you have both sets of descriptions for each situation. Your Assistant should have only the Counselor descriptions.

2. Call for your first counselor volunteer: "We need a female counselor for a group of 12-year-old girls..." Once you know the volunteer, we like to give the counselor a big introduction—"Here now to play the Counselor, a 5-year camp veteran, from Columbus, Ohio...."—and then lead the audience in a loud round of applause. At the end of the role-play, we will thank all participants and applaud again.

3. Your Assistant then escorts the Counselor out of the room into a "soundproof booth." While there, the Assistant will read to the volunteer the situation description labeled for the Counselor.

4. Once they have left the room, introduce the Camper: "I would like you to meet Jane Doe. She's a 12-year-old camper...." Now read both situation descriptions to the entire staff. "Here's what the Counselor knows.... And here's the full-story from the Camper's perspective...."

5. Call for the Assistant to bring the Counselor back into the room.

6. Almost all of the situations begin with an opening line from the Camper.

7. The Camper should keep the pace moving. The situation should run several minutes with the Camper slowly giving ground to the Counselor.

8. As the Moderator, you will gain a feel for when to end the role-play. We like to end with "Thank you. Let's clap it up for our volunteers."

9. Begin the debriefing.

STEP THREE
Debriefing the Situations

At the debriefing of the first situation, you may want to reiterate any ground rules presented at the start of the activity (or beginning of orientation) regarding how we support all ideas and how much you respect everyone who participates. Camp is all about participation.

We like to begin with the following question: "Who can tell me some things that the volunteer did well?" If no hands go up (they usually do), call on a few key staff you know will provide some positive feedback. In leading the discussion, you may want to ask some of the following questions:

Ask the Counselor:

1. How did you think that went?
2. What was the most challenging part?
3. What would you do differently?
4. Did you feel obligated to speak?
5. Did you feel you needed help at any point?

Ask the Audience:

1. Did the Counselor clearly understand the heart of the situation and respond accordingly?
2. How was the Counselor's emotional mood going into the situation?
3. Did the Counselor get frustrated when there was no progress?
4. How did the Counselor leave things?
5. What suggestions might you have for the Counselor?

Ask the Camper:

1. What did the Counselor say that made you feel like he/she was listening to you?

2. When did the counseling turn the corner for you?

3. What did you like about the way that the Counselor talked to you?

4. What would you have liked the Counselor to do?

Make sure you reinforce key points of what the Counselor did do right or offer suggestions to improve for next time. "I like the way you got down at eye level and reassured them…" "Next time, don't promise to keep a secret…" "Make sure you are having this conversation in clear view of everyone…" "A clearer way to explain your point would be to say…"

Counselors will eventually develop their own lingo, but for counselors who are just starting out or for veteran counselors looking for new ways to explain their point of view, we have included a list of helpful phrases at the end of this chapter.

As the Moderator, you will positively acknowledge each suggestion. Sometimes you may want to tweak an answer so that it aligns with camp philosophy or how you would want a counselor to respond. Keep the pace of the session moving by taking only 4-5 responses to each question.

You then wrap up the role-play by providing the camp's perspective. More often than not, you will find that the staff has already covered the main ideas on how you would want to handle the situation. This is especially so as they gain experience with this particular training session. Keep your summary short, maybe three or so talking points.

Some General Thoughts on Debriefing the Situations

Over time, some general approaches for working with children emerge, and we thought it would make sense to highlight a few here:

- **Stabilize the Situation** (sometimes easier said than done in real life). Give the campers time to compose themselves. You want to listen to what they have to say, but need for them to calm down a bit. Give them time to do this, staying a small distance away. In real life, this may take 15 minutes (or much longer). For the purpose of the role-playing, time accelerates. Acknowledge this to the audience and let them know that it is very difficult to reason out a problem with an extremely upset camper. How to calm down an upset camper is something you will want to cover during staff training.

- **Listen to the Camper**. Get down to their level and make eye contact. If there's anything learned from these role-playing exercises is that counselors usually do not have all the information as to what is upsetting the camper.

- **Thank the Camper** for sharing with you.

- **Share Your Own Experience** from your camper life or when growing up.

- Without being demeaning, **Know the Value of Humor.**

- Know when to tell the camper that you should go together to **Get Help.**

TIPS AND TECHNIQUES FOR SPEAKING WITH CAMPERS

- Get on their eye-level.
- Use the camper's name.
- Avoid reprimand in front of peers; take campers aside.
- Ask them what's wrong.
- Listen to them.
- Validate their emotions ("It must be upsetting when…").
- Share the experience with a personal anecdote.
- Assure the camper that they can belong and contribute.
- Praise actions they did that were helpful.
- Build a relationship (refer to common experiences or activities/interests they like).
- Separate the behavior from the person ("I like you; I just don't like what you did.").
- Clarify their choices.
- Teach them how to move forward (how to express their anger, manage their fear, and communicate with their peers).
- Map out consequences.
- Smile.
- Talk calmly and avoid repeating yourself.
- Use physical touch (shoulder, upper arm, middle of upper back) to reassure them.
- Provide them with a clean slate and a chance to rejoin the group.

100 HELPFUL PHRASES

Listed below are some useful phrases to help you to redirect the camper or to move on to the next topic if you feel like your conversation with them is going in circles.

1.   A better way to say that/do that the next time might be to…

2.   Change takes time, but it also takes some effort on your part. Do you think you are ready?

3.   Does this happen to you at home? What do your parents say/do?

4.   Do you know what is going to happen to you if we can't resolve this problem?

5.   Do you like it here? Why/Why not?

6.   Do you like it when people treat you this way? Why do you think they are treating you like this?

7.   Do you mind if we play cards/jacks/shoot baskets while we talk?

8.   Do you see how people are treating you differently? Do you want them to treat you like that?

9.   Don't be afraid to ask for help. Find a counselor.

10. Don't hold grudges. Sometimes you just have to let go.

11. Don't underestimate yourself.

12. Every day I want you to celebrate your accomplishments. No accomplishment is too small. Each time you don't lose your temper, that's progress. Each time you share with your

bunkmates, that's progress. Each time you celebrate your successes, that's progress.

13. This is a part of camp. When you come to camp you have to help out/clean up/follow the rules/go to activities.

14. When you do (action), this happens….

15. Everyone messes up once in a while. That's okay. How you reacted was not okay. Here's what you can do next time.

16. Have I treated you unfairly?

17. Hitting is not an option. It is unacceptable. Period.

18. I admire you. I think you have great leadership skills. Maybe one day you will be sitting where I am as a counselor talking to a camper like yourself. What would you say to that camper to make them feel better?

19. I believe you.

20. I bet if you think about it for a while, you'll come up with a solution.

21. I can see you're not ready to talk right now. Let me know when you're ready and I'll be happy to listen.

22. I have asked you in a respectful way to stop (name the behavior) and you have refused. Why?

23. I know it feels tough right now, but it gets better. I believe in you even when you don't believe in yourself."

24. I like it better when you (state the desired behavior).

25. If you let me finish talking, I promise to give you a turn and listen to everything you have to say.

26. I like you. You're a great kid. But when you say/do those things, it makes it hard for people to want to be around you.

27. I need your help.

28. I see that you are unhappy. What I am trying to understand is why you are trying so hard to let everyone know.

29. I think we can fix this, but I'm going to need your help.

30. I think we may need to talk to your Group Leader/the Head Counselor/the doctor/your parents to get some advice/help.

31. I think you owe someone an apology.

32. I want to be here for you. Tell me how I can help you.

33. I want to help you.

34. I want to thank you for being so honest with me. It helps me to understand what is really going on and makes it easier for me to find a solution for you.

35. I wonder what would happen if....

36. I would prefer it if you ask first.

37. I'm going to ask you to live in the moment and not worry about the past or the future.

38. I'm going to describe a couple of different scenarios. You stop me when it sounds like if fits this situation.

39. I'm not being mean to you. I warned you that if you kept [action], this would happen. When you chose to [action], this is what is going to happen as a result.

40. I'm not sure if you are understanding my point. Let me put it this way...

41. I'm so proud of you!

42. I'm sorry.

43. I'm surprised you did that. You're such a good kid. That's not something you normally do, is it?

44. If you can't decide, would it make it easier for me to make the decision for you.

45. Is there anything we could have done differently, to prevent this from happening?

46. Is there anything you could have done differently, to prevent this from happening?

47. Is this how you want to be remembered? What you want campers and counselors to think about you?

48. It's like there are two of you. One that everyone enjoys hanging out with and the one who makes these mistakes.

49. It's not easy admitting when we are wrong. I had to do it the other day when I...

50. It's okay to be angry, but that doesn't mean you have to do angry things.

51. It's okay to be scared/angry/frustrated. Everyone feels that way at some time.

52. It's okay to express yourself, but that kind of talk is not okay here at camp.

53. Let me see if I understand you correctly. Is this what you are saying...? (summarize their point of view)

54.   Let's figure out something fun for you to do today.

55.   Let's figure out something nice you can do for the group/for this person to show them that you are willing and able to make a fresh start.

56.   Let's get to the bottom of this. What are the facts?

57.   Let's pretend that yesterday never happened. Would you like to hear how we can have a fresh start?

58.   Let's work out a signal so that you can secretly let me know when you need to give yourself a break from the group before you melt down.

59.   Look at your friend. He's crying. What you did made him cry. How does that make you feel? Friends don't do that to each other.

60.   Maybe if I gave you some examples of similar things you've said/done that would help give you a better understanding....

61.   Maybe people are treating you like that because that's the way you treat them.

62.   Maybe people treat you like that because of the way you are acting.

63.   Maybe you don't know, but we don't do/say that here.

64.   Nothing happened this time, but what if something were to go wrong and someone got hurt? How would you feel?

65.   Sharing is a part of friendship.

66.   So are you telling me that you aren't willing to even try this?

67. Sometimes I need help when I don't know what to do? I may have a solution that can help you. Would you like to hear it?

68. Sometimes talking about what you are feeling is hard. Would you prefer to have some time to write down your thoughts?

69. Sometimes the hardest things to do are the most important to help solve a problem.

70. Tell me the moment it happens. It's easier to address a problem while it's still fresh in people's minds.

71. Thank you for telling me.

72. That doesn't make any sense to me.

73. That's okay to think that/feel that. Now let's figure out a way for you to let us know that is what you are thinking/feeling.

74. There is a better way for you to handle this the next time it comes up.

75. This is a lot of information for me to process. Do you mind if we take a break so I can think about this for a little while? Thank you.

76. This is going to sound crazy…but…

77. This is not good, but let's try to make it better.

78. This is not my area of expertise, but I know someone else who knows a lot about this and can really help…

79. This isn't safe.

80. We have talked enough for now. We need to go on to the next step.

81. What can we do to resolve this situation and make everyone feel better?

82. What if someone did this to you?

83. What if they are not doing it on purpose? Does that change anything?

84. What would you do if you were in my shoes?

85. What's your favorite/least favorite thing about camp?

86. Why do you think people are mean to you/don't want to hang out with you?

87. Would you say/do this in front of your parents/ grandparents?

88. Wow! That was scary/weird/crazy!

89. You are absolutely right, and….

90. You are not a bad person. You just made a bad choice.

91. You are too old/too young to be doing things like that.

92. You can't always control what happens to you, but you can control how you react to what happens.

93. You can't always control what other people do, but you can control how you respond to them.

94. You don't have to be friends with everyone. Just treat everyone with respect.

95. It doesn't seem like you listened to a word I said yesterday. You're getting in trouble for the same thing. What's going on?

96. You need to accept responsibility for your actions. That begins by apologizing for what you did. And then I want you to come up with a fair way to make things right between you and (person).

97. You need to stop that now. We don't allow that here.

98. You're not going to believe this, but that happened to me too one time.

99. You're not going to like hearing this… but…

100. You're really good at (activity). I bet you can help me come up with a solution.

ADDITIONAL WAYS TO USE ROLE-PLAYING

OPTION 1: Put Yourself In Their Shoes

In addition to role-playing as a Counselor, feel free to role-play as a Group Leader, Head Counselor, or Camp Owner.

OPTION 2: Show How It's Not Done

Demonstrate a scenario with bad counseling, and then add a new Counselor with redirection to a more positive result.

OPTION 3: Breakout Sessions

Use them as breakout sessions to cover age or gender specific issues.

OPTION 4: With Campers

Use role-playing with campers when a division is having trouble getting along. Have them switch roles and role-play the Counselor to see how they would have handled the situation.

About The Role-Playing Cards

The next two sections contain the role-playing situations divided into Girls' Side Situations and Boys' Side Situations. For each role-play you will need a matching pair of cards:

- one for the **Moderator** (containing both the Camper and Counselor situations), and

- one for the **Assistant** (containing only the Counselor situation).

We have laid the cards out for you so that each situation can be photocopied onto an 8 1/2 x 11 inch of piece of paper or cardstock and then cut in half.

The Situations

GIRLS' SIDE SITUATIONS

Camper-Camper Conflicts

HATES CAMP

Female Camper, 9 years old

Counselor (volunteer):

One of your first-year campers has withdrawn from the group. She hides out in the bunk at Rest Hour and she has written 5 letters home all marked "Urgent." Find out what's going on. You speak first.

First Line: "I was going to mail your letters and noticed that all five of them had no stamp…. and were marked urgent. What's so urgent?"

New Camper (9 years old):

You are upset because all the returning kids have been bossing you about. They also run off to do things and never include you. You are tired of all the inside jokes and comments ("remember last year when we…" or "so and so was so funny last year when…"). You hate camp and want to leave. The counselor speaks first.

Second Line: "I wanna go home."

HATES CAMP

Female Camper, 9 years old

Counselor (volunteer):

One of your first-year campers has withdrawn from the group. She hides out in the bunk at Rest Hour and she has written 5 letters home all marked "Urgent." Find out what's going on. You speak first.

First Line: "I was going to mail your letters and noticed that all five of them had no stamp…. and were marked urgent. What's so urgent?"

STEALING

Female Camper, 9 years old

Counselor (volunteer):

Something strange is afoot. Several of your campers and indeed campers in other divisions too claim that they never received packages their parents sent. Rachel was the first camper to suspect someone was opening other people's packages and stealing the contents. Some of your campers have done some detective work on their own and believe that Rachel is the thief. Find out what she knows.

Camper (9 years old):

Unlike your bunkmates, it is a financial struggle for you parents to send you to camp. Because it was going to be a financial stretch for them, they told you that they wouldn't be able to send any care packages to you. The first package you stole and opened was so that you could have candy. But once you got away with the first one, it was hard to stop. Recently you opened a package that had a cell phone in it. As the pile of candy and toys grew, it became harder to hide them. You've recently started hiding them under your counselor's bed in her suitcase. If she accuses you of stealing them, accuse her right back and tell her you have proof. If she corners you, ask for a way to save face and give back what you took.

First Line: "Did you catch the thief yet"

STEALING

Female Camper, 9 years old

Counselor (volunteer):

Something strange is afoot. Several of your campers and indeed campers in other divisions too claim that they never received packages their parents sent. Rachel was the first camper to suspect someone was opening other people's packages and stealing the contents. Some of your campers have done some detective work on their own and believe that Rachel is the thief. Find out what she knows.

CAMPER TOOK INAPPROPRIATE PHOTOS

Female Camper, 10 years old

Counselor (volunteer):

You have received some complaints from girls in your group that one of their bunkmates was using her PSP to take pictures of everyone changing for General Swim. Some of the girls don't mind. They even did silly poses. But others did mind. And to make matters worse, you've overheard her say that she plans to upload them to her Facebook account when she gets home. You ask to see her.

Camper (10 years old):

Just before camp your grandmother gave you a PSP. One feature is the ability to take photos and to apply all sorts of special effects. You have been taking all sorts of silly photos, including some of your friends running around the bunk naked. These will be so hilarious when you upload them to your Facebook page when you get home. Just in the middle of tagging your favorite pictures, your counselor asks to talk to you about your photos. Assure her that you know how to change the Facebook privacy settings so only your friends can see them. Tell her that back home you send photos like this to your friends using your cell phone, and that it's no big deal

First Line: *"I didn't do it. Whatever it was....uh... You wanted to see me?"*

CAMPER TOOK INAPPROPRIATE PHOTOS

Female Camper, 10 years old

Counselor (volunteer):

You have received some complaints from girls in your group that one of their bunkmates was using her PSP to take pictures of everyone changing for General Swim. Some of the girls don't mind. They even did silly poses. But others did mind. And to make matters worse, you've overheard her say that she plans to upload them to her Facebook account when she gets home. You ask to see her.

Female Camper, 10 years old

CAMPER WALKS OFF

Counselor—Group Leader (volunteer):

One of your campers is often getting into arguments and even some fights. She is teased frequently and when she teases back, it always escalates badly. This camper is clearly unhappy. You see her sitting alone and decide it is a good time to have a conversation about what's going on. As you approach her, you have the first line....

First Line: "Can a talk with you for a minute...."

Camper (10 years old):

You are not having a good time at camp. Your bunkmates tease you, and when you tease back an argument or a fight always breaks out. This often happens right in front of your counselors who are reading or napping on their beds and they do nothing except occasionally yell to be quiet. Your Group Leader wants to talk to you (again!) about fighting. You feel she isn't solving anything. You are miserable and don't want to be here anymore. As your Group Leader approaches you, you've had enough. After she speaks her first line, you respond and walk away from her.

Second Line: "I'm going home and you can't stop me."
[literally walk away from her.]

CAMPER WALKS OFF

Female Camper, 10 years old

Counselor—Group Leader (volunteer):

One of your campers is often getting into arguments and even some fights. She is teased frequently and when she teases back, it always escalates badly. This camper is clearly unhappy. You see her sitting alone and decide it is a good time to have a conversation about what's going on. As you approach her, you have the first line....

First Line: "Can a talk with you for a minute...."

Female Camper, 10 years old

WON'T DO ACTIVITY-1

Counselor (volunteer):

Today is the first full day of camp and your group has Tower for the first period. Part of the reason parents send their children to camp is so they can try new things. Consequently, before the end of the session you would like each of your campers to give climbing a try. All of your campers have willingly attempted to climb to the top of the Tower. All but one. Karen. At first Karen refuses to even put on the harness and helmet. There's 15 minutes left in the period, it's hot, and the rest of the group is annoyed with her and is starting to call her names. You tell the climbing instructor to choose some volunteers to go a second time, while you meet separately with Karen.

Camper (10 years old):

Today is your first full day at a sleepaway camp. The first activity of the day is Tower. You are not scared of heights, but you have never climbed before. You're a slow learner and you are nervous about looking foolish in front of your new friends as you try to make it to the top. You would rather not attempt climbing in front of them. Hopefully you can try it during an Optional period. Unfortunately, the group has started making fun of you and even your counselor is making a scene and insisting that you try. If this is what your summer is going to be like, you want to go home. Insist on calling your parents so they can pick you up.

First Line: *"This sucks. I wanna call my parents!"*

WON'T DO ACTIVITY-1

Female Camper, 10 years old

Counselor (volunteer):

Today is the first full day of camp and your group has Tower for the first period. Part of the reason parents send their children to camp is so they can try new things. Consequently, before the end of the session you would like each of your campers to give climbing a try. All of your campers have willingly attempted to climb to the top of the Tower. All but one. Karen. At first Karen refuses to even put on the harness and helmet. There's 15 minutes left in the period, it's hot, and the rest of the group is annoyed with her and is starting to call her names. You tell the climbing instructor to choose some volunteers to go a second time, while you meet separately with Karen.

INAPPROPRIATE COMMENTS

Female Camper, 10 years old

Counselor (volunteer):

Some campers in your division have mentioned that a girl in the division often makes inappropriate comments when everyone is changing for General Swim. Some thought she was just hacking around, because when she got changed she would pretend she was a stripper and do a funny dance as she got undressed. Then one day, you overhear this camper bragging during a ceramics class that she knows all about sex and that she learned it from her stepfather. You ask her to step outside onto the deck of the Ceramics cabin. You are in clear view of everyone else but just out of earshot. Talk to her about her behavior.

Camper (10 years old):

Your counselor pulls you out of a Ceramics class to talk to you about some comments you made where you said you knew all about sex. What's the big deal? Everyone's father or step-father gives their daughter the sex talk and shows them what to do so they won't be scared their first time. Your stepfather has made you promise to keep this information a secret, which you never understood, because if everyone gets the same talk, then it is not a secret. Now you are worried your counselor is going to call your parents and tell them that you told the secret. You are frightened that you'll get in trouble. Get your counselor to promise not to tell the camp director.

First Line: "Am I in trouble?"

INAPPROPRIATE COMMENTS   Female Camper, 10 years old

Counselor (volunteer):

Some campers in your division have mentioned that a girl in the division often makes inappropriate comments when everyone is changing for General Swim. Some thought she was just hacking around, because when she got changed she would pretend she was a stripper and do a funny dance as she got undressed. Then one day, you overhear this camper bragging during a ceramics class that she knows all about sex and that she learned it from her stepfather. You ask her to step outside onto the deck of the Ceramics cabin. You are in clear view of everyone else but just out of earshot. Talk to her about her behavior.

TWO CAMPERS IN THE SAME TOILET STALL   2 Female Campers, 10 years old

Counselor (volunteer):

You enter the bunk and hear whispering in the bathroom. You sneak closer and hear that there are two voices coming from the same stall. From what you overhear it sounds like they are doing something very inappropriate. You knock on the door and ask them to come out. There is panic on the other side of the door, and it sounds like they are struggling to get their clothes on. You knock again, and demand they come out immediately. You need to get to the bottom of this immediately. When they appear...

Campers 1 & 2 (10 years old):

You are trying to make a birthday card to surprise your counselor on her birthday tomorrow, but she is always around. The two of you are hiding in one of the bunk toilet stalls drawing the card, when your counselor knocks on the stall door and asks the two of you to come out. You make excuses while you nervously try to hide the supplies down your shorts. Admit to nothing. Deny nothing. Say nothing. Refuse to give any information. Keep your secret safe as long as you can.

First Line (Camper 1): "I thought I had a tick and she was helping me check."
Camper 2: Turns out it was a false alarm. Okay, bye.

TWO CAMPERS IN THE SAME TOILET STALL 2 Female Campers, 10 years old

Counselor (volunteer):

You enter the bunk and hear whispering in the bathroom. You sneak closer and hear that there are two voices coming from the same stall. From what you overhear it sounds like they are doing something very inappropriate. You knock on the door and ask them to come out. There is panic on the other side of the door, and it sounds like they are struggling to get their clothes on. You knock again, and demand they come out immediately. You need to get to the bottom of this immediately. When they appear...

Female Camper, 10 years old

WHINING CAMPER

Counselor (volunteer):

You've just figured out why all camps have screens on all the windows… it's to prevent counselors from throwing campers through the windows. Case in point: Whining Wendy. All day long, all she does is complain about everything. "It's too hot. I hate pasta. Why do we have to clean up. I want ice cream, not pretzels!" and so on and so on. Not only are the campers fed up, but you are too. In an attempt to cheer her up you brought her a cup of lemonade, which—no surprise—she hates and proceeds to smack it out of your hands onto the ground.

Camper (10 years old):

Why is everyone around you so stupid? It seems like you have to explain everything to them. It's simple: you love snacks and drinks that are sweet and not sour or salty. You will eat M&Ms but not the ones that are red, yellow or orange. You hate having to wear t-shirts and sneakers with socks. You'd rather wear a tank top and sandals. It's really annoying that people can't remember what you like. Your counselor in an attempt to cheer you up brought you a cup of your least favorite drink in the world—lemonade—even though you have repeatedly told her that you HATE lemonade. You smack it to the floor.

First Line: "You know I hate lemonade. Are you stupid or something?"

WHINING CAMPER

Female Camper, 10 years old

Counselor (volunteer):

You've just figured out why all camps have screens on all the windows… it's to prevent counselors from throwing campers through the windows. Case in point: Whining Wendy. All day long, all she does is complain about everything. "It's too hot. I hate pasta. Why do we have to clean up. I want ice cream, not pretzels!" and so on and so on. Not only are the campers fed up, but you are too. In an attempt to cheer her up you brought her a cup of lemonade, which—no surprise—she hates and proceeds to smack it out of your hands onto the ground.

CLIQUE

Female Camper, 11 years old

Counselor (volunteer):

One of your first-year campers wants to go home. Talk to her and find out why.

Camper (11 years old):

You are upset, because all the returning kids have been bossing you about. They also run off to do things and never include you. Sometimes they're even mean about it. [Example: When you asked them to join in their game of jacks, they chanted, "Tick tock the game is locked and no one can come in."] You are tired of all the inside jokes and comments ("Remember last summer when we…" or "So and so was so funny last year when…" You want to hang out with a specific group of girls, but they don't wan to hang out with you. This feels nothing like the camp promotional video where friends are hanging out together having a good time.

First Line: "I want to go home."

CLIQUE

Female Camper, 11 years old

Counselor (volunteer):

One of your first-year campers wants to go home. Talk to her and find out why.

Female Camper, 11 years old

EARLY BLOOMER

Group Leader (volunteer):

You are the Group Leader in charge of a group of 11-year-old girls. One of your campers has suddenly become quite popular with the boys this year. It might be because between last summer and this summer, she grew breasts. She seems anxious about tonight's Social. She has just finished talking to your co-counselor (a JC), and now wants to talk to you. See what she wants.

Camper (11 years old):

You are the first in your group to go through puberty and are the only one who has to wear a bra. Ever since you grew breasts, you have been getting a lot of attention from the boys in your matching division. They never gave you the time of day the first three years they knew you, but now they do. Some of them are pressuring you to let them touch "under the shirt, over the bra." Ask your Group Leader how many dates do you have to go one before you let them do this. And how about "under the shirt, under the bra"? You don't want to endanger your newfound popularity by refusing their requests too long. You don't want to be a tease, but you also don't want to give in too early. You don't want to be like the JC in your division, who told you she always goes all the way on the first date. Ask your Group Leader for advice.

First Line: "Can I ask you a question, woman to woman?"

EARLY BLOOMER

Female Camper, 11 years old

Group Leader (volunteer):

You are the Group Leader in charge of a group of 11-year-old girls. One of your campers has suddenly become quite popular with the boys this year. It might be because between last summer and this summer, she grew breasts. She seems anxious about tonight's Social. She has just finished talking to your co-counselor (a JC), and now wants to talk to you. See what she wants.

OUTCAST

Female Camper, 11 years old

Counselor (volunteer):

A first-year camper comes up to you crying and tells you that no one likes her. You have seen her butt into conversations, race ahead to always be first in line, cracks stupid jokes, talks too loud, etc. She's a bit of a know it all, etc. She comes to you, because no one wants to be her buddy at General Swim. You've been waiting for an opportunity to talk to her on how she can get along better with her bunkmates.

Camper (11 years old):

This is your first summer at camp and no one in your bunk wants to hang out with you. Whenever you go up to a couple of bunkmates who are chatting and try to join in, they walk away. You think that they just don't want anyone new in their little clique. Now at General Swim, you can't go into the water unless you have a buddy, and nobody wants to buddy up with you. You are fed up with being frozen out. You go to speak to your counselor:

First Line: *"The other girls in the division are acting like stuck-up snotty little bitches, and I'm sick of it!"*

OUTCAST

Female Camper, 11 years old

Counselor (volunteer):

A first-year camper comes up to you crying and tells you that no one likes her. You have seen her butt into conversations, race ahead to always be first in line, etc. She's a bit of a know it all, cracks stupid jokes, talks too loud, etc. She comes to you, because no one wants to be her buddy at General Swim. You've been waiting for an opportunity to talk to her on how she can get along better with her bunkmates.

Female Camper, 11 years old

WON'T DO AN ACTIVITY

Counselor (volunteer):

A camper in your group (11 years old) never wants to do soccer. Every time soccer is scheduled, it is a battle to get her to join in the activity. Convince her to do the activity.

Camper (11 years old):

You're not a good runner. You feel like you are overweight. You don't want to look stupid in front of your bunkmates—a lot of whom are very good athletes. The first time you played soccer this year, no one passed you the ball. After the game, they all talked about how many goals they had scored.

First Line: ***"I'm not doing soccer. Soccer sucks."***

WON'T DO AN ACTIVITY

Female Camper, 11 years old

Counselor (volunteer):

A camper in your group (11 years old) never wants to do soccer. Every time soccer is scheduled, it is a battle to get her to join in the activity. Convince her to do the activity.

WON'T SHARE

Female Camper, 11 years old

Counselor (volunteer):

You are a counselor for a division of 11-year-old girls. One of your campers refuses to share anything with her bunkmates. Not candy, not toys, not anything. She won't even let people sit on her bed. What's worse is the rest of the bunks want her moved to another cabin. Help her find a way to repair her relationships with her bunkmates.

Camper (11 years old):

You are an only child and you have never had to share. You are very particular about your belongings. You have nice things and you take very good care of them. You have a policy of never borrowing or lending. If one of your bunkmates likes your hair straightener, then they can write to their parents and get their own. Additionally, you never share your candy or let people sit on your bed. When people complain you say, "Don't Share. Don't Care." They think your little chant is very obnoxious. Your bunkmates had a not-so-secret vote and they no longer want you in their cabin. It's within your rights not to have to share. You think your counselor is a hypocrite. As proof ask to borrow her cell phone or her pearl earrings. Tell her you overheard her tell another counselor that she doesn't lend out her car. Convince her your point of view is a valid one.

First Line: **"Don't Share. Don't Care."**

WON'T SHARE

Female Camper, 11 years old

Counselor (volunteer):

You are a counselor for a division of 11-year-old girls. One of your campers refuses to share anything with her bunkmates. Not candy, not toys, not anything. She won't even let people sit on her bed. What's worse is the rest of the bunks want her moved to another cabin. Help her find a way to repair her relationships with her bunkmates.

Female Camper, 12 years old

SAD CAMPER

Counselor (volunteer):

Every time you turn around you see one of your campers talking a counselor's ear off about how sad she is. Everyone listens patiently and offers helpful advice such as to keep active, write home, hang out with friends, etc. She's not homesick and there don't seem to be any issues from home. Nothing seems to be wrong, but nothing seems to be working. She's still "sad." Word has gotten to you that on more than one occasion she has threatened to kill herself. One day you overhear her say that she wishes she were dead. You go over to her and ask to join you on a bench nearby on campus so that you can talk to her.

Camper (12 years old):

This is your 3rd year of camp and you feel like you don't fit in. The activities are okay, but you don't really have a favorite activity. Your friends are nice, but all they seem to talk about these days is boys, which you find boring. Your parents don't want you home, and you don't care where you spend your summer as long as you can be somewhere where people care about you. Sometimes you wish you were dead, then maybe people would seem to care more about you and what you liked. Your counselor overhears you saying you'd like to kill yourself, and wants to talk to you.

First Line: **"Oh my god. Don't tell me you're going to make a big deal of all of this. I was just kidding."**

SAD CAMPER

Female Camper, 12 years old

Counselor (volunteer):

Every time you turn around you see one of your campers talking a counselor's ear off about how sad she is. Everyone listens patiently and offers helpful advice such as to keep active, write home, hang out with friends, etc. She's not homesick and there don't seem to be any issues from home. Nothing seems to be wrong, but nothing seems to be working. She's still "sad." Word has gotten to you that on more than one occasion she has threatened to kill herself. One day you overhear her say that she wishes she were dead. You go over to her and ask to join you on a bench nearby on campus so that you can talk to her.

TALENT SHOW HECKLER

Counselor (volunteer):

During the big 4th of July Talent Show, you notice one of your campers making fun of a girl camper attempting to sing "Tomorrow" from *Annie*. In all honesty she is pretty bad, but this is what she loves to do. Twice you've motioned to the disruptive camper to be respectful, but both times she went back to cracking jokes to her bunkmates: "I wish it was tomorrow, because then we wouldn't have to hear her singing that awful song!" Her jokes are getting louder and louder and are now causing a disruption. After the song, you pull her outside the theatre to talk to her.

Camper (12 years old):

At the start of every summer you are forced to sit through one of the most excruciating events in the history of summer camps—the Talent Show, which is ironic because there is very little talent in the show. You come to camp for the sports. It's bad enough you are forced to waste your time doing things like arts and crafts, but then to have to sit through a talent shows is sheer torture. On stage now is a girl attempting to sing "Tomorrow" from the musical *Annie*. Not only do you think the song is stupid, but her rendition is painful. So you crack jokes to your bunkmates, which they find hilarious. By the way this is the same girl who, when you're playing in the big camp Basketball Tournament, doesn't pay attention and talks through the game. Why should you respect what she does, if she doesn't respect what you do?

First Line: "Oh my God! Thank you for rescuing me! This Talent Show sucks!"

Female Camper, 12 years old

TALENT SHOW HECKLER

Female Camper, 12 years old

Counselor (volunteer):

During the big 4th of July Talent Show, you notice one of your campers making fun of a girl camper attempting to sing "Tomorrow" from *Annie*. In all honesty she is pretty bad, but you know that she loves singing and this is what she wants to do when she grows up. Twice you've motioned to the disruptive camper to be respectful, but both times she went back to cracking jokes to her bunkmates: "I wish it was tomorrow, because then we wouldn't have to hear her singing that awful song!" Her jokes are getting louder and louder and are now causing a disruption. After the song, you pull her outside the theatre to talk to her.

Female Camper, 12 years old

NAME CALLER

Counselor (volunteer):

One of your campers (12 years old) is sitting by herself looking miserable. You have heard a rumor that she had a falling out with Nancy, one of her bunkmates. You got wind about some teasing going on (this camper kept calling her Fancy Nancy, which she didn't like), but you didn't step in, because you thought they should be able to resolve the issue themselves. See if you can help make things right.

Camper (12 years old):

There is a girl in your division, Nancy, who just bothers you. She always thinks she's right, she never shares but always mooches off other people, she gossips about your friends, she always pushes in front to be first.... You have taken to calling her "Fancy Nancy," because you think she is stuck up. She has made it known that it bothers her when you call her that, but in your mind, she deserves it. One day, she couldn't take your teasing anymore and has instructed everyone to freeze you out. Since then, no one will hang out with you or talk to you. When you ask them a question, they answer curtly and walk away. Or sometimes they just ignore you. You are miserable and don't know what to do. You are too embarrassed to talk about it to anyone, but you feel if you don't talk about it, the rest of the summer is going to be even more depressing. You don't really want to go home. You want things to be they way they were before, except without Nancy being so selfish or pushy.

First Line: "*Leave me alone. I don't want to talk.*"

NAME CALLER

Female Camper, 12 years old

Counselor (volunteer):

One of your campers (12 years old) is sitting by herself looking miserable. You have heard a rumor that she had a falling out with Nancy, one of her bunkmates. You got wind about some teasing going on (this camper kept calling her Fancy Nancy, which she didn't like), but you didn't step in, because you thought they should be able to resolve the issue themselves. Apparently they didn't. See if you can help make things right.

Female Camper, 12 years old

NOT EATING

Counselor (volunteer):

You notice one of your campers has been eating less and less. In fact, at lunchtime she didn't eat anything. She's lost several pounds this week and is starting to look unhealthy. She hates looking at herself in the mirror. Your sister had anorexia and you know how serious a disease it can be. The hardest part of her illness was admitting that she had an eating disorder. There was no mention on her confidential about any issues with eating. But she is 12, so maybe she is starting to feel self-conscious or embarrassed about the changes her body is going through.

Camper (12 years old):

Just before camp you cheated on one of your final exams in school. Someone else got caught and you let them take the blame. As a result, their punishment was that they couldn't go away to camp that summer. You are feeling really guilty. You can't stand the sight of yourself in the mirror. You've been eating less and less at meals and have lost several pounds. The guilt is gnawing at you, but you don't want to tell anyone, because you are afraid you will be sent home. You love camp, and don't want to be sent home, because all your friends are here. Life is an internal Hell at the moment. At lunch you don't eat anything, and your counselor asks to talk to you.

First Line: **"You wanted to see me?"**

NOT EATING

Female Camper, 12 years old

Counselor (volunteer):

You notice one of your campers has been eating less and less. In fact, at lunchtime she didn't eat anything. She's lost several pounds this week and is starting to look unhealthy. She hates looking at herself in the mirror. Your sister had anorexia and you know how serious a disease it can be. The hardest part of her illness was admitting that she had an eating disorder. There was no mention on her confidential about any issues with eating. But she is 12, so maybe she is starting to feel self-conscious or embarrassed about the changes her body is going through.

TAMPON DEMONSTRATION

Female Camper, 12 years old

Counselor (volunteer):

You're hanging out in your bunk during Rest Hour writing a letter to a friend back home, when you hear one of your campers say, "Who wants to learn how to put in a tampon?" Anyone interested is to follow her to the Shower House where she is going to show how to properly put in a tampon. She grabs a big pink box of tampons from under her bed and asks you if you wouldn't mind supervising and helping out anyone who is having trouble.

Camper (12 years old):

You were the first girl in your division to get your period, something you are very proud about. You can't wait to share your newfound knowledge about menstruation, so you announce to your bunk that you are going to the Shower House to demonstrate to your bunkmates how to correctly insert a tampon. You grab a large box of tampons (containing enough for everyone) and are about to leave when you notice your counselor staring at you. Since she is supervising the bunk during Rest Hour, and everyone is going to the Shower House for your little workshop, invite her along.

First Line: "Hey wanna join us? You can supervise and help out anyone who is having trouble."

TAMPON DEMONSTRATION

Female Camper, 12 years old

Counselor (volunteer):

You're hanging out in your bunk during Rest Hour writing a letter to a friend back home, when you hear one of your campers say, "Who wants to learn how to put in a tampon?" Anyone interested is to follow her to the Shower House where she is going to show how to properly put in a tampon. She grabs a big pink box of tampons from under her bed and asks you if you wouldn't mind supervising and helping out anyone who is having trouble.

Female Camper, 13 years old

BED PLACEMENT

Counselor (volunteer):

One of your campers (13 years old) comes to you with a bed placement request. She doesn't like where she is sleeping. She doesn't like the campers on either side of her. Truth be told, no one in the bunk likes this camper and they refuse to sleep next to her. Also, there is no room in the other bunk in the division, so that's not an option either. Find a solution that will make both the bunk and the camper happy.

Camper (13 years old):

You don't like where you are sleeping and demand to be moved. You hate the people on either side of you and don't get along with them. You'd rather sleep next to your counselor, but that's where all the "cool kids" are sleeping. If your counselor won't move you, you want to go home.

First Line: "I hate where I'm sleeping. I want to sleep on the other side of the bunk."

BED PLACEMENT

Counselor (volunteer):

One of your campers (13 years old) comes to you with a bed placement request. She doesn't like where she is sleeping. She doesn't like the campers on either side of her. Truth be told, no one in the bunk likes this camper and they refuse to sleep next to her. Also, there is no room in the other bunk in the division, so that's not an option either. Find a solution that will make both the bunk and the camper happy.

Female Camper, 13 years old

Female Camper, 13 years old

NOT A HAPPY CAMPER

Counselor (volunteer):

Your camper (13 years old) is very unhappy. She refuses to hang out with her bunkmates. Figure out what's wrong and make her feel better.

Camper (13 years old):

You can't focus on having fun at camp, because your parents have just decided to split up. You're embarrassed about your situation at home and don't really want anyone to know.

First Line: **"I want to call home. Let me talk to my parents. I want to go home."**

NOT A HAPPY CAMPER

Counselor (volunteer):

Your camper (13 years old) is very unhappy. She refuses to hang out with her bunkmates. Figure out what's wrong and make her feel better.

Female Camper, 13 years old

SOCIAL

Female Camper, 13 years old

Counselor (volunteer):

One of your campers (13 years old) won't go to the coed Social. Talk to her and find out why. She can't stay in the bunk, because there will be no supervision. Convince her to go.

Camper (13 years old):

You absolutely don't want to go to this evening's coed Social, because you got dumped at the last Social and you will be the only one without a boyfriend. You can't face an evening of everyone asking you what happened.

First Line: *"Save your breath. I'm not going."*

SOCIAL

Female Camper, 13 years old

Counselor (volunteer):

One of your campers (13 years old) won't go to the coed Social. Talk to her and find out why. She can't stay in the bunk, because there will be no supervision. Convince her to go.

HATES CAMP

Counselor (volunteer):

One of your Campers (14 years old) has withdrawn from the group. She hides out in the bunk at Rest Hour and she has written a letter home marked "Urgent." Find out what's going on.

First Line: "I was going to mail your letter and noticed that it was marked urgent. What's so urgent?"

Female Camper, 14 years old

New Camper (14 years old):

You are upset because your bunkmates are always running off to do things and never include you. This feels nothing like the last two years of camp when you were all in the same bunk having fun. You are tired of all the inside jokes and comments like ("That outfit looks horrible on you," "Are you really wearing that?", "Well, I was Athlete #1 four years in a row, of course I'm the best at sports," etc...). Or things like ("You really look fat. Just kidding" or "I can't believe she gave her boyfriend a hand job; she's such a slut.") You hate camp and want to leave.

Second Line: "I'm going home on Visiting Day."

HATES CAMP

Female Camper, 14 years old

Counselor (volunteer):

One of your Campers (14 years old) has withdrawn from the group. She hides out in the bunk at Rest Hour and she has written a letter home marked "Urgent." Find out what's going on.

First Line: "I was going to mail your letter and noticed that it was marked urgent. What's so urgent?"

HOMESICKNESS

Female Camper, 14 years old

Counselor (Volunteer):

For the past week, one of your first-year campers has spent all her free time (cleanup, Rest Hour, after Taps) at the Health Center. She claims to have chronic stomach pains. It's 9:30 P.M. at night. She's just asked to go to the Health Center again. Some of her bunkmates are getting fed up about her ducking out of cleanup and activities she doesn't want to do.

Camper: (14 years old)

It's your first year away at camp and you get stomachaches periodically during the day. Your stomach doesn't really hurt at activities, just when you have free time or are by yourself. Going to the Health Center seems to make you feel better. You may be homesick, but you don't know because you've never felt this way before and you've never been away from home before. Also, you may not want to admit it if it is true, because you are 14 years old, and only little kids get homesick. Right?

First Line: [it's 9:30 P.M. at night] *"Can I go to the Health Center?"*

HOMESICKNESS

Female Camper, 14 years old

Counselor (Volunteer):

For the past week, one of your first-year campers has spent all her free time (cleanup, Rest Hour, after Taps) at the Health Center. She claims to have chronic stomach pains. It's 9:30 P.M. at night. She's just asked to go to the Health Center again. Some of her bunkmates are getting fed up about her ducking out of cleanup and activities she doesn't want to do.

Female Camper, 14 years old

OD NIGHTMARE

Counselor (volunteer):

A bunk of 14-year-old girls has come to you in an uproar. They are fed up with one of their bunkmates, because she plays her music too loud at night and they hate her music. They want her out of the group, and ask you for help. You go to the camper to work out a solution and find out what is going on.

First Line: "Hi [name]. Can I talk to you for a minute?"

Camper (14 years old):

You like to play your music at night really loud. Bunkmates are complaining. You don't care, because you have just as much right to play your music as the next person. Your bunkmates are fed up with you. You don't care. You don't like them, and they don't like you. You pay the same tuition to be there as everyone else. Just because nobody likes your music doesn't mean you shouldn't get to play it. Your bunkmates don't like anyone to be different, and by complaining about you, they are trying to bully you into conforming. The more they complain, the louder you make the music.

OD NIGHTMARE

Female Camper, 14 years old

Counselor (volunteer):

A bunk of 14-year-old girls has come to you in an uproar. They are fed up with one of their bunk-mates, because she plays her music too loud at night and they hate her music. They want her out of the group, and ask you for help. You go to the camper to work out a solution and find out what is going on.

First Line: "Hi [name]. Can I talk to you for a minute?"

BULLYING

Female Camper, 14 years old

Counselor (volunteer):

You have gotten wind that one of your 14-year-old campers has been bullying Kate, one of her bunkmates. She only does it when there are no counselors around. She coats her poisonous barbs in humor. She'll tell Kate she looks ugly, and then follows it up with "Just kidding." You've also heard that Kate is being frozen out of the group. She does other things to Kate too, such as pretending Kate is invisible, ignoring her when she talks, or making eye contact, laughing and then walking away. Kate has always been super nice to everyone. Talk to her and find out why she is being so mean to Kate.

Camper (14 years old):

Nobody seems to get your sense of humor. The other day when you and your bunkmates were getting ready for a Social, you told your friend Kate (who by the way is dating a boy you liked), that you thought she looked fat. But then you quickly followed it up by saying, "Just kidding." Now she's upset with you. She complained to your counselor that you are being mean to her. As an example, she quotes the fact that you and your friends make eye contact with her, laugh, and then walk away. She also claims that you are rounding up other bunkmates to freeze you out. You can hang out with whomever you choose. Just because you are bunkmates doesn't mean you have to be friends. You think she should just lighten up and learn how to take a joke. By the way, Kate stole your boyfriend.

First Line: "Can you talk to Kate? She is so annoying."

BULLYING

Female Camper, 14 years old

Counselor (volunteer):

You have gotten wind that one of your 14-year-old campers has been bullying Kate, one of her bunk-mates. She only does it when there are no counselors around. She coats her poisonous barbs in humor. She'll tell Kate she looks ugly, and then follows it up with "Just kidding." You've also heard that Kate is being frozen out of the group. She does other things to Kate too, such as pretending Kate is invisible, ignoring her when she talks, or making eye contact, laughing and then walking away. Kate has always been super nice to everyone. Talk to her and find out why she is being so mean to Kate.

Camper-Counselor Conflicts

Female Camper, 8 years old

EXPLOSIVE CHILD

Counselor (volunteer):

You are relaxing in your bunk on a period off when a Junior Counselor tells you that one of your campers "melted down" in Arts and Crafts and is now sitting on the porch of the HC waiting to talk to you. You are told she was asked to leave, because she was screaming and using abusive language. She called the A&C counselor a "big fat ugly cow" and told her to "Go to Hell!" This is not the first time you have had to talk to her about losing her temper. It takes very little to set her off. Give her some advice to help her.

Camper (8 years old):

No one listens to you and when they do, they don't really "get it." You never get to have your way. You can't wait until you are bigger so you can boss other people around. You are in trouble because at arts and crafts you melted down and kept screeching at the top of your lungs. "I need the glue NOW. I said NOW otherwise THIS WILL BE RUINED!!! IT'S NOT FAIR!!!!" If they just gave you the glue, none of this would have happened. You feel you are being treated unfairly because you always go last or have to wait your turn only because you are the youngest and shortest person in the division.

First Line: *"Shut up. I don't want to talk to you right now!!!"*

EXPLOSIVE CHILD

Female Camper, 8 years old

Counselor (volunteer):

You are relaxing in your bunk on a period off when a Junior Counselor tells you that one of your campers "melted down" in Arts and Crafts and is now sitting on the porch of the HC waiting to talk to you. You are told she was asked to leave, because she was screaming and using abusive language. She called the A&C counselor a "big fat ugly cow" and told her to "Go to Hell!" This is not the first time you have had to talk to her about losing her temper. It takes very little to set her off. Give her some advice to help her.

Female Camper, 9 years old

I THINK I LIKE YOU—1

Counselor (volunteer):

One of your 9-year-old campers is a lot of fun. You had fun hanging out at first, but now she is always there. You never feel you have any privacy. And then there are the presents or the little notes.   At first it was cute, but now it's getting a little creepy. You think she has a crush on you, which is confirmed when you come back to the bunk at Rest Hour and find her lying in your bed under the covers. Ask to speak to her outside, making sure you are in full view of others.

Camper (9 years old):

You have the best counselor in camp! She is everything you want to be when you grow up—good looking, fun, smart, a good athlete, adventurous.... Whenever you hang around with her you have the best time. She seems to enjoy hanging out with you. You make her presents in arts and crafts and share your food with her. One day during Rest Hour, you are lying in her bed seeing what the World must look like from her perspective, when she asks to see you outside on the porch. You are excited to have some special one-on-one time with your favorite counselor.

First Line: "This is so cool! What do want to chat about?"

I THINK I LIKE YOU—1

Female Camper, 9 years old

Counselor (volunteer):

One of your 9-year-old campers is a lot of fun. You had fun hanging out at first, but now she is always there. You never feel you have any privacy. And then there are the presents or the little notes. At first it was cute, but now it's getting a little creepy. You think she has a crush on you, which is confirmed when you come back to the bunk at Rest Hour and find her lying in your bed under the covers. Ask to speak to her outside, making sure you are in full view of others.

Female Camper, 10 years old

INSOMNIA

Counselor (volunteer):

One of your campers keeps waking you up in the middle of the night saying she can't sleep. She doesn't seem homesick. She doesn't cry during the day. But at night she has trouble sleeping. What's helped in the past is just talking to her for 30 minutes until she falls asleep. However, she doesn't wake any other counselor up, just you. You are losing sleep and getting really cranky during the day. You dread going to bed, because you know just when you've fallen asleep, she's going to wake you up again. And it seems to take longer and longer for her to fall asleep. Last night you almost talked until dawn. Try a different strategy the next time she wakes you.

Camper (10 years old):

Back home, whenever you can't sleep, you go to your parents' room and wake them up. Your mom lets you sleep in bed with them and rubs your back and talks to you until you fall asleep. You're having some sleepless nights. You've been waking up your favorite counselor to see if she can help you fall back asleep. She's starting to get annoyed though. You're lonely and you miss the affection your family gives you. Ask your counselor if she can lie on your bed until you fall asleep. Talking doesn't seem to help anymore. Insist she do it.

First Line: "I can't sleep."

INSOMNIA

Female Camper, 10 years old

Counselor (volunteer):

One of your campers keeps waking you up in the middle of the night saying she can't sleep. She doesn't seem homesick. She doesn't cry during the day. But at night she has trouble sleeping. What's helped in the past is just talking to her for 30 minutes until she falls asleep. However, she doesn't wake any other counselor up, just you. You are losing sleep and getting really cranky during the day. You dread going to bed, because you know just when you've fallen asleep, she's going to wake you up again. And it seems to take longer and longer for her to fall asleep. Last night you almost talked until dawn. Try a different strategy the next time she wakes you.

Female Camper, 10 years old

OVERWEIGHT CAMPER

Counselor (volunteer):

One of your campers (10 years old) is overweight. On Sally's confidential the parents disclosed that they wanted their child to lose weight this summer. They want her to exercise during Rest Hour and Free Play and eating junk food is strictly forbidden. Naturally, she hates to exercise and loves to eat candy. When you walk into the bunk at Rest Hour, you see Sally all alone gorging on junk food. Convince the camper to stop eating and to play an activity outside.

First Line: "Hey there [camper], what are you doing? We just ate lunch."

Camper (10 years old):

You are ten years old and overweight. Maybe some of this is baby fat, but some is definitely from lack of exercise and from a poor diet. You tend to go on eating binges whenever you are sad. Your grandmother has been sick for the last year, which is when you really started putting on weight. You just got a phone call from home saying that Grandma is very ill. You handle your grief the only way you know how—by binging. You're not in the mood to socialize or do anything. You just want to sit by yourself and eat. Unless your counselor has a better way to deal with the sadness, this one is working just fine. Counselor speaks first.

Second Line: "Leave me alone. It's my food; I can eat it whenever I want to."

OVERWEIGHT CAMPER

Female Camper, 10 years old

Counselor (volunteer):

One of your campers (10 years old) is overweight. On Sally's confidential the parents disclosed that they wanted their child to lose weight this summer. They want her to exercise during Rest Hour and Free Play and eating junk food is strictly forbidden. Naturally, she hates to exercise and loves to eat candy. When you walk into the bunk at Rest Hour, you see Sally all alone gorging on junk food. Convince the camper to stop eating and to play an activity outside.

First Line: "Hey there [camper], what are you doing? We just ate lunch."

Female Camper, 10 years old

THE CAST LIST

Counselor (volunteer):

You notice a camper (10 years old) check the newly posted cast list for the play and then walk away crying. You go over to the camper to talk to her.

Camper (10 years old):

You have just checked the bulletin board and once again you have discovered that you didn't get the part that you wanted in the camp play. Once again you have a tiny part singing in the chorus. You only have one line in the entire play. You feel upset, because every year the same kids get all the best roles. Even though you are not as good as the other kids, drama is the one thing you like. You think the drama counselor is being unfair and you want to quit the play.

First Line: "Camp sucks."

THE CAST LIST

Counselor (volunteer):

You notice a camper (10 years old) check the newly posted cast list for the play and then walk away crying. You go over to the camper to talk to her.

Female Camper, 10 years old

WON'T GO ON OVERNIGHT

Female Camper, 10 years old

Counselor (volunteer):

Your group is about to go on their big overnight of the summer and just before setting off one of your campers springs it on you that she absolutely won't go on the overnight. She'd rather sleep in the bunk by herself, which of course she can't do, because there would be nobody to supervise her, as all the counselors will be on the overnight. The group is getting impatient waiting. Convince her to go on the overnight.

Camper (10 years old):

You grew up in New York City and are not a big fan of "roughing it." Your division is going on an overnight tonight and you absolutely do not want to go on it. You don't mind having a camp-fire in the woods, but the idea of sleeping in a tent or going to the bathroom in the woods is out of the question. Lie, exaggerate, cry. Do whatever you need to do to get out of going on the overnight.

First Line: "Save your breath. I'm not going on the overnight."

WON'T GO ON OVERNIGHT

Female Camper, 10 years old

Counselor (volunteer):

Your group is about to go on their big overnight of the summer and just before setting off one of your campers springs it on you that she absolutely won't go on the overnight. She'd rather sleep in the bunk by herself, which of course she can't do, because there would be nobody to supervise her, as all the counselors will be on the overnight. The group is getting impatient waiting. Convince her to go on the overnight.

FEAR OF WATER—WON'T SWIM

Female Camper, 11 years old

Counselor (volunteer):

It is the first day of camp and your group's first activity is to take a required swim test. All the girls in your group are excited about swimming in the lake and are getting changed. One of your campers refuses to take the test or even to get into a bathing suit. She is lying on her bed looking unhappy. You tell your co-counselor to take the group swimming so you can see if you can convince her to do her swim test.

Camper (11 years old):

This is your first day at a sleepaway camp. In accordance with camp policy, you have to take a swim test with your group. You don't want to change in front of your bunkmates or take the swim test for a couple of weeks, because you have some embarrassing bruises around your genital area. If questioned, lie about where they came from (i.e., experimented with inserting a tampon or you slipped while riding your bike ...). You don't want anyone to know they are from your 13-year old cousin. You're afraid that if someone finds out, you'll be sent home, and you also don't want to get your cousin in trouble. You ultimately will share this information with the counselor, but do what you can to make sure the counselor doesn't tell anyone else.

First Line: "I'm not going, and you can't make me."

FEAR OF WATER—WON'T SWIM

Female Camper, 11 years old

Counselor (volunteer):

It is the first day of camp and your group's first activity is to take a required swim test. All the girls in your group are excited about swimming in the lake and are getting changed. One of your campers refuses to take the test or even to get into a bathing suit. She is lying on her bed looking unhappy. You tell your co-counselor to take the group swimming so you can see if you can convince her to do her swim test.

Female Camper, 11 years old

REFUSES TO DO CLEANUP

Counselor (volunteer):

Campers in your division are complaining that one of their bunkmates is refusing to clean the bathroom every time it's her turn. They don't think it's fair. See if you can convince her to pitch in.

Camper (11 years old):

Back home you have a housekeeper who makes your bed, tidies your room, and cleans your bathroom. Your counselors can tell you until they are blue in the face that everyone has to pitch in, but you absolutely refuse to clean up the bathroom. You think it's disgusting. You shouldn't have to do it; that's what cleaning people are for. If the camp wants the bathroom and the bunk tidy, they should hire some people to do it. And if they can find some that are not too lazy, those people can do a good job. Should your counselor try to make you clean up, threaten that you will call your parents to have them fired. If your counselor says that your parents didn't hire her, so they can't fire her, remind her that your camper tuition pays her paycheck.

First Line: **"Don't even waste your time. I'm not cleaning that bathroom!"**

REFUSES TO DO CLEANUP

Female Camper, 11 years old

Counselor (volunteer):

Campers in your division are complaining that one of their bunkmates is refusing to clean the bathroom every time it's her turn. They don't think it's fair. See if you can convince her to pitch in.

Female Camper, 12 years old

ACTIVITY OUT OF CONTROL

Counselor (volunteer):

On your period off you went to make a phone call and discovered you had 50 text messages and even more voicemail messages, all congratulating you on the upcoming birth of your child. Others wanted to know who the father is or about the due date. You quickly scroll through the sent messages and see that the following message was sent to everyone in your address book: "I just wanted everyone to know that I'm pregnant." You have been playing pranks on your campers and they have been playing pranks back, but this is too far. You find out which camper was the mastermind behind the prank and you go to talk to her.

Camper (12 years old):

As a practical joke you and some of your bunkmates steal your counselor's phone and text everyone in her address book the following message: "I just wanted everyone to know that I'm pregnant." If she gets offended, too bad. There's no way you're going to apologize. You weren't the one that started the pranks. Your counselor is always playing practical jokes on all of you (like when she pretended she got fired—which was really upsetting), so now it's payback time. You can't wait to see her reaction. There is no way she won't find this funny.

First Line: "*So, do you know yet if it's going to be a boy or a girl?*"

ACTIVITY OUT OF CONTROL

Female Camper, 12 years old

Counselor (volunteer):

On your period off you went to make a phone call and discovered you had 50 text messages and even more voicemail messages, all congratulating you on the upcoming birth of your child. Others wanted to know who the father is or about the due date. You quickly scroll through the sent messages and see that the following message was sent to everyone in your address book: "I just wanted everyone to know that I'm pregnant." You have been playing pranks on your campers and they have been playing pranks back, but this is too far. You find out which camper was the mastermind behind the prank and you go to talk to her.

Female Camper, 13 years old

DISRUPTIVE CAMPER

Counselor (volunteer):

One of your campers (13 years old) keeps clowning around during tennis. Her disruptive behavior is annoying the rest of the group as well as the tennis counselors. For example, she jokes around when the tennis staff is giving instructions, she hits tennis balls over the fence on purpose, and during the drills and games, she hacks around and spoils it for everyone. When you confront her, she says she is just having fun and what's the big deal. You tell her that if she acts out one more time, she will have to sit down. She has acted out once more, and so you pull her out to talk to her.

Camper (13 years old):

You are not good at tennis, and you don't want to look stupid in front of your bunkmates—a lot of whom are very good athletes. The only way you can have fun is to joke around. This appears to annoy your counselor. You've told her to lighten up and that you are just having some fun. She has pulled you out of the activity and wants to talk to you.

First Line: "What's the big deal? I come to camp to have fun, and I'm having fun."

DISRUPTIVE CAMPER

Female Camper, 13 years old

Counselor (volunteer):

One of your campers (13 years old) keeps clowning around during tennis. Her disruptive behavior is annoying the rest of the group as well as the tennis counselors. For example, she jokes around when the tennis staff is giving instructions, she hits tennis balls over the fence on purpose, and during the drills and games, she hacks around and spoils it for everyone. When you confront her, she says she is just having fun and what's the big deal. You tell her that if she acts out one more time, she will have to sit down. She has acted out once more, and so you pull her out to talk to her.

GAY COUNSELOR

Counselor (volunteer):

You are a very popular at camp. You are smart, funny, athletic, good looking, and an amazing counselor. You are also gay. You are "out" to your friends and family at home, and to one or two of your closest friends at camp, but you never talk about your personal life with your campers. One day, out of the blue, the camper, who sleeps next to you, has asked your Group Leader to be moved to another spot in the bunk. She used to call you her favorite counselor and look up to you, but now she is avoiding you and acting a little weird. Find out what's wrong.

First Line: "*You look a little down. Is everything okay?*"

Female Camper, 13 years old

Camper (13 years old):

You found out that the counselor who sleeps next to you is gay. You discovered this by reading a letter that was lying on her shelf. She used to be your favorite counselor but now that you found this out, you are extremely weirded out by it. Up until now, she has been your role model—she is smart, funny, athletic, good looking, and an amazing counselor. Somehow being gay, in your mind, seems to cancel out all of that. Your parents wouldn't want your role model to be someone gay. You have asked your Group Leader to move you to the other side of the bunk for "personal reasons," but your Group Leader told you that you are old enough to resolve them by talking with her. You are sitting along on a bench outside of the bunk when you see the counselor approaching.

GAY COUNSELOR

Counselor (volunteer):

You are a very popular at camp. You are smart, funny, athletic, good looking, and an amazing counselor. You are also gay. You are "out" to your friends and family at home, and to one or two of your closest friends at camp, but you never talk about your personal life with your campers. One day, out of the blue, the camper, who sleeps next to you, has asked your Group Leader to be moved to another spot in the bunk. She used to call you her favorite counselor and look up to you, but now she is avoiding you and acting a little weird. Find out what's wrong.

First Line: "You look a little down. Is everything okay?"

Female Camper, 13 years old

INAPPROPRIATE QUESTION

Female Camper, 13 years old

Counselor (volunteer):

It's Rest Hour and the girls are quietly reading an article called "How to Perform Great Oral Sex" in *Cosmopolitan* magazine. When you enter the bunk, conversation quickly shifts to this topic and one of the campers starts asking you about sex.

Camper (13 years old):

You have been dating one of the Senior Boys for three weeks. He has been hinting at moving the relationship to the next level, and you feel you might be ready. You have just read an article about "How to Perform Great Oral Sex" in Cosmopolitan magazine and you want to relentlessly interrogate your counselor about her sexual experiences. Get as many details as possible.

First Line: "Have you ever given your boyfriend a blowjob"?

INAPPROPRIATE QUESTION

Female Camper, 13 years old

Counselor (volunteer):

It's Rest Hour and the girls are quietly reading an article called "How to Perform Great Oral Sex" in *Cosmopolitan* magazine. When you enter the bunk, conversation quickly shifts to this topic and one of the campers starts asking you about sex.

Female Camper, 13 years old

ALWAYS LAST

Counselor (volunteer):

The Activity Bugle blew and it's time to go to Basketball. Everyone is out of the bunk except Sue. She is always the last person out of the bunk. That is unless the activity is arts and crafts. You love sports and are starting to resent that you're the one who always has to hang back and try to get Sue out of the bunk. She dawdles so slowly that oftentimes you miss half the activity. It's not fair to you or to the other campers, who really enjoy when you join in and play basketball with them. You need to put an end to this behavior now. Tell Sue to get her act together and get to activities on time.

Camper (13 years old):

This is your 3rd year at camp. You've never liked sports. You'd much rather focus your talents on your creative skills, of which you have many. This year, however, you have a problem. One of your counselors is a bit of a jock and talks very condescendingly about the Arts, which you love. Because she derides those activities and talks up the sports, she has convinced some of your closest friends to not waste their time "making crap out of popsicle sticks" and learn some sports that will "make them popular." She is not only taking away your friends, but she is also taking away any chance you have of standing out in the group. You decide to make her life as miserable by taking longer and longer to get ready for sport activities. You want her to miss out on something she loves so she can feel how you feel. If she insinuates you're lazy, tell her (insincerely)

First Line: "What? I'm going as fast as I can."

ALWAYS LAST

Female Camper, 13 years old

Counselor (volunteer):

The Activity Bugle blew and it's time to go to Basketball. Everyone is out of the bunk except Sue. She is always the last person out of the bunk. That is unless the activity is arts and crafts. You love sports and are starting to resent that you're the one who always has to hang back and try to get Sue out of the bunk. She dawdles so slowly that oftentimes you miss half the activity. It's not fair to you or to the other campers, who really enjoy when you join in and play basketball with them. You need to put an end to this behavior now. Tell Sue to get her act together and get to activities on time.

CAUGHT USING SOMEONE'S CELL PHONE

Female Camper, 14 years old

Counselor (volunteer):

You are walking back to your cabin at night and you hear a camper talking to herself. As you get closer you see the distinctive glow of a cell phone. It is against camp policy for campers to have a cell phone. Confiscate the phone.

Camper (14 years old):

You want to talk to some of your friends back home, so you ask to borrow a cell phone from one of your bunkmates, who has hidden hers successfully all summer. Her last instruction to you was, "Just don't get caught." Midway though your phone call, your counselor catches you. Beg, plead, threaten—do whatever you have to so that the counselor doesn't turn you in or take away the cell phone. It's one thing to get in trouble for using the cell phone, but you don't want your bunkmate to get in trouble too.

First Line: (to person on the other end of the cell phone call) "Oh crap. Gotta go."

CAUGHT USING SOMEONE'S CELL PHONE

Female Camper, 14 years old

Counselor (volunteer):

You are walking back to your cabin at night and you hear a camper talking to herself. As you get closer you see the distinctive glow of a cell phone. It is against camp policy for campers to have a cell phone. Confiscate the phone.

Female Camper, 14 years old

SELF HARM

Counselor (volunteer):

One of your campers who has been a little depressed has stopped going to General Swim. On two occasions, you asked her if anything was wrong and she assured you that she was fine. Today you notice some scratches on her thighs. Talk to her.

Camper (14 years old):

You are someone who has high standards and you put a lot of pressure on yourself. As a Tribe Leader you are feeling very stressed. You're afraid that your team's songs and final projects won't be good enough to win a first or second prize at the end of the summer. You have stolen an X-acto knife blade from arts and crafts and have begun to make small cuts on your thighs just under where your shorts cover. Initially it temporarily eases the stress. Afterwards you feel angry with yourself and regret doing it. But you know no other way to make yourself feel better.

First Line: "If this is about the Sing Plaque, I know I can fix the lettering with a little paint."

SELF HARM

Female Camper, 14 years old

Counselor (volunteer):

One of your campers who has been a little depressed has stopped going to General Swim. On two occasions, you asked her if anything was wrong and she assured you that she was fine. Today you notice some scratches on her thighs. Talk to her.

CAMPER DOESN'T LIKE INSTRUCTOR

Female Camper, 15 years old

Counselor (volunteer):

Your star player (15 years old) wants to quit the basketball team. While she is the strongest player technically, she is not a very generous player on the court. She almost never passes the ball, even when someone else has a better chance at making the shot. Your goal has always been to give the weaker players game time to give them experience and coaching to strengthen their skills. Your star player doesn't see it that way. She sees it as acts of charity that is hurting the team's chances at winning a lot of trophies. You are attempting to build them into a team. She doesn't see that, because she is not a team player. She asks to speak to you.

Camper (15 years old):

You don't like your counselor who is coaching you in basketball. She seems more focused on developing the skills of the players on the bench than in winning games. Several times she has pulled you out of the game when your team was up "to give other players a chance to play." You don't think those players take the game as seriously as you do and are frustrated with your teammates. But the real blame falls with your coach, who you feel is not competitive enough. It's not enough to win. You want to win by a large margin, and you believe you can be instrumental in helping the team slaughter the competition. If her approach is going to be "everyone plays so everyone grows," then tell her you want to quit. If she presses you, tell her you don't like her as a coach.

First Line: *"I just wanted you to know that I am quitting the team."*

CAMPER DOESN'T LIKE INSTRUCTOR

Counselor (volunteer):

Your star player (15 years old) wants to quit the basketball team. While she is the strongest player technically, she is not a very generous player on the court. She almost never passes the ball, even when someone else has a better chance at making the shot. Your goal has always been to give the weaker players game time to give them experience and coaching to strengthen their skills. Your star player doesn't see it that way. She sees it as acts of charity that is hurting the team's chances at winning a lot of trophies. You are attempting to build them into a team. She doesn't see that, because she is not a team player. She asks to speak to you.

Female Camper, 15 years old

INAPPROPRIATE QUESTION

Female Camper, 15 years old

Counselor (volunteer):

You are hanging out with one of your campers chatting about this and that and conversation shifts to tonight's Social.

Camper (15 years old):

You have a camp boyfriend who you have been hinting at that you are ready to go all the way. You are both virgins and you don't want to be embarrassed that you'd do it wrong. You have a Social tonight, and if all goes right, you and your boyfriend are planning on sneaking off to hook up. Your older sister lost her virginity at camp and you don't want to go home unless you do too. You want to ask your counselor for advice. Begin by innocently asking what time tonight's Social begins, then by asking her the name of her first boyfriend, and then ask her about when she lost her virginity. Prod her for tips and advice.

First Line: "What time are we heading down to the Social?"

INAPPROPRIATE QUESTION

Female Camper, 15 years old

Counselor (volunteer):

You are hanging out with one of your campers chatting about this and that and conversation shifts to tonight's Social.

Female Camper, 15 years old

OVER-ACHIEVER

Counselor (volunteer):

One of your campers (15 years old) has been a camp leader throughout her camp career. She has always been voted Captain of the Baseball and Basketball teams. She was very much looking forward to the ultimate honor in her camp career—being voted Color War Captain. Knowing her leadership, you know that she is a shoe-in for the honor. You hear an unofficial report that she was voted Color War Captain. Congratulate her and give her some advice about what you learned when you were a Color War Captain.

First Line: **"Congratulations! I heard you are going to be a Color War Captain."**

Camper (15 years old):

You have had a memorable camp career. You captained many baseball and basketball teams, you were the lead in almost all of the shows, etc. This summer will be your final year as a camper. There was only one achievement left that would make your camp career perfect—to be a Color War Captain like your mother and grandmother. Unfortunately when your division voted, you didn't receive enough votes to become Captain. This has devastated you. You are angry with your division for not voting for you and disappointed with yourself for not getting to be a Color War Captain. You are terrified to tell your parents that you didn't get voted Captain. You have disgraced and humiliated them. You are scared, hurt, and confused. The counselor has the first line.

Second Line: **"I hate this place, and I hate you!"**

OVER-ACHIEVER

Female Camper, 15 years old

Counselor (volunteer):

One of your campers (15 years old) has been a camp leader throughout her camp career. She has always been voted Captain of the Baseball and Basketball teams. She was very much looking forward to the ultimate honor in her camp career—being voted Color War Captain. Knowing her leadership, you know that she is a shoe-in for the honor. You hear an unofficial report that she was voted Color War Captain. Congratulate her and give her some advice about what you learned when you were a Color War Captain.

First Line: "Congratulations! I heard you are going to be a Color War Captain."

Female Camper, 15 years old

STOLEN GOODS

Counselor (volunteer):

You get back from your big divisional trip and you find out that one of your campers (15 years old) stole a "Please Wait to be Seated" sign from the mall and nailed it to one of the bathroom stall doors. Even though no one will say who did it, you were able to find out that she was the one who went to woodshop to borrow a hammer and nails. Tell her you are going to make her return it, apologize, and then tell her she will not be able to attend the big, year-end coed camp party. This was the punishment agreed on by you with the Head Counselor.

Camper (15 years old):

The big trip this year was to some lame Shakespeare production in the woods. Couldn't have been more boring. At the mall, to liven things up, your friend steals a "Please Wait to be Seated" sign from the restaurant where you ate. You thought it would look hilarious on your bathroom stall door back at the bunk. The moment you get back you get a hammer and nails from woodshop and put it up. Your counselor notices it and wants to speak to you. Make sure you don't rat on your friend. Except, if they threaten a severe punishment.. Then change your story and say who really did it.

First Line: "Oooo...Great trip. Who knew Hamlet could be so fascinating?"

STOLEN GOODS

Female Camper, 15 years old

Counselor (volunteer):

You get back from your big divisional trip and you find out that one of your campers (15 years old) stole a "Please Wait to be Seated" sign from the mall and nailed it to one of the bathroom stall doors. Even though no one will say who did it, you were able to find out that she was the one who went to woodshop to borrow a hammer and nails. Tell her you are going to make her return it, apologize, and then tell her she will not be able to attend the big, year-end coed camp party. This was the punishment agreed on by you with the Head Counselor.

Female Camper, 15 years old

WALL OF SILENCE

Counselor (volunteer):

You notice one of your campers is missing. You look for her and find her at the campfire site smoking a cigarette. This is a major violation of camp policy and you are obligated to report it to your Head Counselor.

Camper (15 years old):

You are smoking a cigarette in the woods during Rest Hour. Your parents don't know you smoke and would be furious with you if they found out. They might even make you come home early from camp. You get caught by one of your counselors. Say, do, or promise anything to prevent this counselor from telling on you, because that'll destroy your whole summer.

First Line: *"Are you going to tell on me?"*

WALL OF SILENCE

Female Camper, 15 years old

Counselor (volunteer):

You notice one of your campers is missing. You look for her and find her at the campfire site smoking a cigarette. This is a major violation of camp policy and you are obligated to report it to your Head Counselor.

Female Camper, 15 years old

EATING PROBLEM

Counselor (volunteer):

One of your campers is not eating at meals. She is thin, but she is obsessed with her weight. You are concerned and talk to your Head Counselor about the issue. The Head Counselor wants you to talk to her about having to eat at every meal.

Campers (15 years old):

Even though on paper you are the weight you are supposed to be, you think you are too fat. You have decided not to eat at meals. When challenged, you may say that this is your body and your choice and it is nobody's business but your own.

First Line: **"You wanted to talk to me."**

EATING PROBLEM

Female Camper, 15 years old

Counselor (volunteer):

One of your campers is not eating at meals. She is thin, but she is obsessed with her weight. You are concerned and talk to your Head Counselor about the issue. The Head Counselor wants you to talk to her about having to eat at every meal.

COUNSELOR DATING CAMPER

Female Camper, 15 years old

Counselor (volunteer):

You bed checked when you came in one night and discovered one of your campers (15 years old) was not in her bed. You conduct a search and find her hanging out on the golf course with her 17-year-old boyfriend. He has been her camp boyfriend for two years, but this is his first year on staff. Break up her little soiree and talk to your camper.

First Line: "What do you think you are doing?"

Camper (15 years old):

You have had a camp boyfriend who is two years older than you are. This summer he is a Junior Counselor and you are still a camper. Several times you have snuck off at night to meet up with your boyfriend when he is off duty. You are boyfriend and girlfriend. You've been dating for two years (since you were 13 and he was 15). Why shouldn't you be allowed to meet up? All the other counselors can hook up at night? There is talk that you won't be allowed to hang out with him during your group's Social Nights. You demand to know why is everything all of a sudden different? Why is everyone all of a sudden treating you like a child? Counselor has first line.

COUNSELOR DATING CAMPER

Female Camper, 15 years old

Counselor (volunteer):

You bed checked when you came in one night and discovered one of your campers (15 years old) was not in her bed. You conduct a search and find her hanging out on the golf course with her 17-year-old boyfriend. He has been her camp boyfriend for two years, but this is his first year on staff. Break up her little soiree and talk to your camper.

First Line: "What do you think you are doing?"

Female Camper, 15 years old

I THINK I LIKE YOU—2

Counselor (volunteer):

One of your campers (15 years old) is looking a little down. For a week, other counselors in the division tried finding out what's wrong, but the camper either refuses to talk or only says, "It's nothing," and walks away. Finally, your camper has come to you and has agreed to talk. You find a picnic table on the edge of campus where you can have some privacy, but are still in full view of everyone.

First Line: *"Thank you for asking to talk to me. We've been worried about you. What's up?"*

Camper (15 years old):

One day you came back to the bunk to brush your teeth and bumped into your counselor stepping out of the shower. You briefly catch a glimpse of her naked. You've seen bunkmates and counselors naked before, but this felt different. It awakened a feeling inside that you've never felt before. Everything about her is beautiful—her body, her smile. You are really confused, because you've only had these kind of feelings for someone of the opposite sex. You can't be sure, but you think you might be gay. You ask to talk to the counselor you have a crush on. Tell her what's been troubling you—that you think you are gay. You're worried that your bunkmates will make fun of you. Once your counselor makes you feel comfortable about the situation, let her know the second part of why you wanted to talk—that you have a crush on her.

Second Line: *"I think I'm gay."*

I THINK I LIKE YOU—2

Female Camper, 15 years old

Counselor (volunteer):

One of your campers (15 years old) is looking a little down. For a week, other counselors in the division tried finding out what's wrong, but the camper either refuses to talk or only says, "It's nothing," and walks away. Finally, your camper has come to you and has agreed to talk. You find a picnic table on the edge of campus where you can have some privacy, but are still in full view of everyone.

First Line: **"Thank you for asking to talk to me. We've been worried about you. What's up?"**

Counselor-Counselor Conflicts

Female CIT, 16 years old

CIT ACTS LIKE CAMPER

Group Leader (volunteer):

You notice one of your CITs abusing her power during a game of "freeze" during lunch. You watch her squirt ketchup on one camper's face, stick a French Fry up another camper's nose, and balance a cup of bug juice on a third camper's head. Call her aside and correct her behavior.

CIT (16 years old):

During a game of "freeze" at lunch time, you squirt ketchup on one camper's face, stick a French Fry up another camper's nose, and balance a cup of bug juice on a third camper's head. You get called out by your Group Leader. It's hypocritical she is yelling at you, because when she was your counselor she did the same thing.

First Line: "Wasn't that hilarious?!!"

CIT ACTS LIKE CAMPER

Female CIT, 16 years old

Group Leader (volunteer):

You notice one of your CITs abusing her power during a game of "freeze" during lunch. You watch her squirt ketchup on one camper's face, stick a French Fry up another camper's nose, and balance a cup of bug juice on a third camper's head. Call her aside and correct her behavior.

IRRESPONSIBLE COUNSELOR

Female Counselor, 18 years old

Counselor (volunteer):

Your first-year counselor is more of a camper than she is a counselor. She takes advantage of her height to push past everyone so that she can be the first to get the food at the seconds table. In the Mess Hall she talks during announcements, she uses freeze games to take her food first and to take more than her share, and is not around during cleanup. And the few times that she has been there, she has slept in her bed. You don't want your whole summer to be like this, so you ask to see her so you can talk to her about her behavior.

Counselor (18 years old):

You are a first-year counselor, and are having the time of your life. You are getting to do all the things your counselors did for/with/to you that made camp fun. For example, in the Mess Hall, you call Freeze and take your food first. During cleanup or during activities you don't like you take a nap. Your co-counselor has asked to see you. By the way, the counselor who is going to berate you was your counselor when your were a camper and there is nothing you are doing that she didn't do her first couple of years as a counselor.

First Line: "Is this about the beer?...No? ...er... You wanted to see me?"

IRRESPONSIBLE COUNSELOR

Female Counselor, 18 years old

Counselor (volunteer):

Your first-year counselor is more of a camper than she is a counselor. She takes advantage of her height to push past everyone so that she can be the first to get the food at the seconds table. In the Mess Hall she talks during announcements, she uses freeze games to take her food first and to take more than her share, and is not around during cleanup. And the few times that she has been there, she has slept in her bed. You don't want your whole summer to be like this, so you ask to see her so you can talk to her about her behavior.

Female Counselor, 19 years old

NEGATIVE ENVIRONMENT

Counselor (volunteer):

The summer started smoothly and everyone in your division has been getting along really well. A few days into camp, a very sarcastic side of one of your counselors has come through. Sometimes her sarcasm is funny, but often it is mean spirited. If a camper spills bug juice at dinner, she says, "Nice one butterfingers. Now clean it up." You overheard her say to the Head Chef (who is bald), "Hey Rogaine, more tater tots. And make sure they're hot this time." Now the campers have adopted her humor based on ridicule, and it has ratcheted up the tension in the bunk. There is much more teasing and fighting. Instead of being cooperative and supportive, they spend their days making nasty snipes at each other. It's time to talk to your counselor about changing her tone.

Counselor (19 years old):

Camp was pretty boring until you showed up to liven things up. Everything was all goody goody nice and supportive. Meal times were peaceful, if by peaceful you mean dull. That's when you decided to open up and treat people to your hilarious sense of humor. Not only are kids laughing at your jokes, but they are even emulating you. Every day becomes more fun than the last as you each try to outdo the other. In the middle of making a hilarious joke about a kid's giant clown feet, your co-counselor has asked to talk to you.

First Line: "Did you see how big that kid's feet are? I bet a family of 4 could live in his shoes!"

NEGATIVE ENVIRONMENT

Female Counselor, 19 years old

Counselor (volunteer):

The summer started smoothly and everyone in your division has been getting along really well. A few days into camp, a very sarcastic side of one of your counselors has come through. Sometimes her sarcasm is funny, but often it is mean spirited. If a camper spills bug juice at dinner, she says, "Nice one butterfingers. Now clean it up." You overheard her say to the Head Chef (who is bald), "Hey Rogaine, more tater tots. And make sure they're hot this time." Now the campers have adopted her humor based on ridicule, and it has ratcheted up the tension in the bunk. There is much more teasing and fighting. Instead of being cooperative and supportive, they spend their days making nasty snipes at each other. It's time to talk to your counselor about changing her tone.

Female Counselor, 19 years old

COUNSELOR LOSES TEMPER

Counselor (volunteer):

During cleanup you leave to bring a camper to the Health Center. You left your co-counselor in charge. Cleanup is your least favorite activity, because your bunk is always a mess, and no one is motivated to do any cleaning. On top of that your co-counselor is always screaming at them, nagging them to go faster, or to do this or that. It's such a drag to be around when she's like that. When you come back from the Health Center, you witness your co-counselor screaming at the messiest camper. You ask to speak to her outside. Maybe you need to remind her that yelling isn't going to make them clean up faster.

Counselor (19 years old):

You share a bunk with one of the laziest counselors you have ever met. She lies on her bed during cleanup, never volunteers to help out or lift a finger or offer up any support or instructions. Not only that, but she finds every excuse possible to avoid being in the bunk. Today she is taking someone to the Health Center. Every day your group is late to first activity, because you are never done with cleanup on time. You are frustrated, because you do all the crappy work, while she goes off and does the fun stuff. She walks in on you as you are trying to break up an argument. She hears you yelling and asks to talk with you. You are furious that she not only continues to duck out, but that she's going to reprimand you on top of everything else.

First Line: "What's up?"

COUNSELOR LOSES TEMPER

Female Counselor, 19 years old

Counselor (volunteer):

During cleanup you leave to bring a camper to the Health Center. You left your co-counselor in charge. Cleanup is your least favorite activity, because your bunk is always a mess, and no one is motivated to do any cleaning. On top of that your co-counselor is always screaming at them, nagging them to go faster, or to do this or that. It's such a drag to be around when she's like that. When you come back from the Health Center, you witness your co-counselor screaming at the messiest camper. You ask to speak to her outside. Maybe you need to remind her that yelling isn't going to make them clean up faster.

ALCOHOL ON COUNSELOR'S BREATH

Female Counselor, 20 years old

Group Leader (volunteer):

One of your campers asks to see you privately. She doesn't want to get anyone in trouble, but she feels she should tell someone. She tells you she bumped into one of her counselors after she came in from a night out celebrating her birthday and was drunk. She said she was really scared, because the counselor was stumbling around, looked confused, and smelled of alcohol. Find the counselor and talk to her.

Co-Counselor (20 years old):

Last night was your birthday. You were not drunk, but you did have several drinks to celebrate. When you came back you bumped into one of your 10-year-old campers who got up in the middle of the night to go to the bathroom. She asked if you had a good birthday, you said you did, she said she was glad you had a good time, and she went back to bed. She has now gone on and told your Group Leader that she bumped into you last night and you were drunk. You were stumbling and that she smelled alcohol on your breath. Now your Group Leader wants to talk to you. You should know that this kid is a bit of a gossip and likes to exaggerate. However, this time her tall tale can get you fired.

First Line: *"You wanted to see me?"*

ALCOHOL ON COUNSELOR'S BREATH

Female Counselor, 20 years old

Group Leader (volunteer):

One of your campers asks to see you privately. She doesn't want to get anyone in trouble, but she feels she should tell someone. She tells you she bumped into one of her counselors after she came in from a night out celebrating her birthday and was drunk. She said she was really scared, because the counselor was stumbling around, looked confused, and smelled of alcohol. Find the counselor and talk to her.

CO-COUNSELOR KEEPS DISAPPEARING

Female Counselor, 20 years old

Counselor (volunteer):

Your Group Leader has split free-time supervision equally amongst the staff so that there is always adequate coverage around the bunks. You have always shown up for your assignment but your co-counselor keeps dodging out of hers. There's always an excuse: "I have to make a phone call," or "I'm just going to check the schedule," or "I'm going to ask if I can borrow someone's racquet." Half the time you end up having to cover her shift. Several times you've seen her ducking into the woods with some other counselors. You're tired of having to pull her weight as well as yours. Just a couple of minutes before her next shift you see her about to duck into the woods. Confront her.

First Line: "Hey, where do you think you're going?"

Counselor (20 years old):

You got a sweet thing going. Your co-counselor is one of those people who follow the Rule Book to the letter. She volunteers for everything and never misses an assignment. And, if you are late for your assignment or are a "no-show," she is so conscientious that she covers your shift for you! Lately, you've been getting high with some friends in the woods. You notice your co-counselor has been getting very stressed (probably from pulling all the extra shifts). Next time you see her, invite her to join you. If she threatens to turn you in, deny, lie, or accuse your way out of it.

Second Line: "I'm going to get high. Wanna join me?"

CO-COUNSELOR KEEPS DISAPPEARING

Female Counselor, 20 years old

Counselor (volunteer):

Your Group Leader has split free-time supervision equally amongst the staff so that there is always adequate coverage around the bunks. You have always shown up for your assignment but your co-counselor keeps dodging out of hers. There's always an excuse: "I have to make a phone call", or "I'm just going to check the schedule," or "I'm going to ask if I can borrow someone's racquet." Half the time you end up having to cover her shift. Several times you've seen her ducking into the woods with some other counselors. You're tired of having to pull her weight as well as yours. Just a couple of minutes before her next shift you see her about to duck into the woods. Confront her.

First Line: "Hey, where do you think you're going?"

CO-COUNSELOR IS USELESS

Female Counselor, 21 years old

Group Leader (volunteer):

You're the Group Leader of a group of 25 nine-year-olds. Here you are again, standing amidst them trying to start an activity, but try as you might, you can't get everyone to settle down. What's worse, is your co-counselor (like always) is just standing there doing nothing. Same thing with cleanup. You can't help it if during cleanup you have to sneak off to the HC to plan upcoming activities. But every time you come back at the end of cleanup, your co-counselor is on her bed reading and the bunk is still a mess. Talk to her and get her to take some initiative of her own. There is no room in this division for lazy counselors.

Counselor (21 years old):

You are a Lower Hill counselor and from day one, your Group Leader has made it clear that she will make all the decisions about scheduling for the group. Even when you've come up with the idea for a fun activity and set it all up for your Group Leader, she never thanks you and even takes the credit when everyone likes it. What's worse is she always disappears at cleanup. She says she is "planning activities," but come on, she can do that the day before or during some of her free time. If she wants to take all the glory, then she should do all the work. So you've done less and less over the past couple of weeks. She now wants to talk to you, and she seems incredibly pissed.

First Line: **"You wanted to see me?"**

CO-COUNSELOR IS USELESS

Female Counselor, 21 years old

Group Leader (volunteer):

You're the Group Leader of a group of 25 nine-year-olds. Here you are again, standing amidst them trying to start an activity, but try as you might, you can't get everyone to settle down. What's worse, is your co-counselor (like always) is just standing there doing nothing. Same thing with cleanup. You can't help it if during cleanup you have to sneak off to the HC to plan upcoming activities. But every time you come back at the end of cleanup, your co-counselor is on her bed reading and the bunk is still a mess. Talk to her and get her to take some initiative of her own. There is no room in this division for lazy counselors.

COUNSELOR SHOUTS TOO MUCH

Female Counselor, 21 years old

Counselor (volunteer):

Campers in your group are complaining that your co-counselor is being mean. You've witnessed her yelling at them to clean up or quiet down. You have a more laid back approach to things. If the bunk isn't totally clean and the beds aren't perfect, it's no big deal. Everything is only going to get messed up again anyway. You think the screaming is not working at all and even you've stopped listening to her. Talk to her and get her to change her approach.

Counselor (21 years old):

You are here not to be some camper's best friend. You are here to be their counselor. In your experience respect is not a given, it's earned. And if you want to be respected you have to be tough. Sometimes that means saying no, and other times it means yelling. Your campers may fear you, but at least they listen to you. Your co-counselor lets them get away with murder. She never corrects them when they do something wrong, so some days are sheer pandemonium. You're starting to tire of her getting to be the nice cop all the time, while you end up looking like the bad cop. If it weren't for you and your "drill sergeant" approach there'd be plenty more fights and cleanup would never get done. Next time you see your co-counselor get her to change her approach to a more rigid one, so that it will be easier to handle the kids.

First Line: "You wanted to see me?"

COUNSELOR SHOUTS TOO MUCH

Female Counselor, 21 years old

Counselor (volunteer):

Campers in your group are complaining that your co-counselor is being mean. You've witnessed her yelling at them to clean up or quiet down. You have a more laid back approach to things. If the bunk isn't totally clean and the beds aren't perfect, it's no big deal. Everything is only going to get messed up again anyway. You think the screaming is not working at all and even you've stopped listening to her. Talk to her and get her to change her approach.

BOYS' SIDE SITUATIONS

Camper-Camper Conflicts

NUDIST

Male Camper, 8 years old

Counselor (volunteer):

Campers in another bunk of your division have come to you to complain about one of their bunk-mates who dances around naked all the time. He's even jokingly "humped" their beds while he was naked or mimed "humping" someone else. They are weirded out by this and are asking you to talk to him.

Camper (8 years old):

This is your first time at sleep away camp, and you were nervous about having to change in front of everyone. Your mother told you that it's normal for boys to change in front of each other and that the naked body is not to be ashamed of. In fact, you should celebrate your body. Her advice maybe helped too much, because you shuck off your clothes every chance you get and dance naked around the bunk. Your exuberance is making some of your bunkmates uncomfortable. They are starting to think you are really weird and want you to stop. You've been pressuring them to dance around naked so they can see how liberating it is. They've refused and have complained to a counselor instead. What's the big deal. There's nothing wrong with being naked right?

First Line: **"Hey this is fun. You should take off your clothes and join in."**

NUDIST

Male Camper, 8 years old

Counselor (volunteer):

Campers in another bunk of your division have come to you to complain about one of their bunk-mates who dances around naked all the time. He's even jokingly "humped" their beds while he was naked or mimed "humping" someone else. They are weirded out by this and are asking you to talk to him.

HE HIT ME, HE HIT ME FIRST

2 Male Campers, 8 years old

Counselor (volunteer):

You walk in on a fight between two 8-year-old campers. Respond.

Camper 1 and Camper 2 (8 years old):

Camper 1 asks Camper 2 to play with one of his electronic toys. Camper 2 is not currently playing with it, but refuses telling him to get his own. Camper 1 called Camper 2 a name. Camper 2 calls Camper 1 a worse name. Camper 1 then hits 2, and Camper 2 hits him back. The two of you are in a middle of a fist fight when you get interrupted.

Camper 1: "He hit me!"
Camper 2: "He hit me first!"

HE HIT ME, HE HIT ME FIRST

2 Male Campers, 8 years old

Counselor (volunteer):

You walk in on a fight between two 8-year-old campers. Respond.

2 Male Campers, 9 years old

BULLYING

Counselor (volunteer):

You notice that one of your campers, who is usually lively, has grown quiet and sullen. He seems to be avoiding one of his other bunkmates. You ask to meet with both of them to see what is going on.

Camper 1/ The Bully (9 years old):

There is a kid in your division you don't like. He never shares his games or his food. So, to teach him a lesson you take them without asking. Whenever he says that he's going to tell on you, you threaten to beat him up. You have hit him before to intimidate him or to punish him for not listening to you. And you know what? It's working. Now when you ask for food or to borrow his toys, he surrenders both quickly and easily.

Camper 2/ The Bullied (9 years old):

You are not happy at camp and want to go home. Camper 1 is being really mean to you and hitting you and you have no idea why.

BULLYING

Counselor (volunteer):

You notice that one of your campers, who is usually lively, has grown quiet and sullen. He seems to be avoiding one of his other bunkmates. You ask to meet with both of them to see what is going on.

2 Male Campers, 9 years old

Male Camper, 9 years old

DISRUPTIVE CAMPER

Counselor (volunteer):

Explain to the group how to play your next activity [make it a simple game such as gaga, spud, or knock out, etc.]

First Line: "*Okay everyone. Listen up. The game we're about to play is called [name of game], and here's how you play....*"

Camper (9 years old)—with several other bunkmates:

Your counselor is about to make you play another boring game that you don't want to play. Keep cracking jokes and interrupting the counselor as he is trying to talk. Be as annoying as possible. If he disciplines you, tell him to "Lighten up!" or "What's the big deal; can't you take a joke?" etc. Counselor speaks first.

DISRUPTIVE CAMPER

Male Camper, 9 years old

Counselor (volunteer):

Explain to the group how to play your next activity [make it a simple game such as gaga, spud, or knock out, etc.]

First Line: *"Okay everyone. Listen up. The game we're about to play is called [name of game] and here's how you play...."*

Male Camper, 9 years old

WON'T SHARE PERSONAL SPACE

Counselor (volunteer):

You hear tension rising on the other side of the bunk and you discover it centers around the fact that one of your campers won't let anyone sit on his bed. For everyone's peace of mind, convince him to just let people sit on his bed. You have pulled him aside to your bed for a one-on-one chat.

First Line: "What's going on over there?"

Camper (9 years old):

You are an only child. You have your own bedroom at home and you've never had to share. Living in a bunk with a dozen other campers is a challenge. You like to keep your bed area neat. You don't like it when other people sit on your bed with their wet bathing suits or dirty shorts or filthy shoes. Your bed is your bed, and you don't understand why people are freaking out that you won't let them sit on your bed. It's your bed and nobody, absolutely nobody, can force you to let people sit on your bed. Counselor speaks first.

WON'T SHARE PERSONAL SPACE

Male Camper, 9 years old

Counselor (volunteer):

You hear tension rising on the other side of the bunk and you discover it centers around the fact that one of your campers won't let anyone sit on his bed. For everyone's peace of mind, convince him to just let people sit on his bed. You have pulled him aside to your bed for a one-on-one chat.

First Line: "What's going on over there?"

Male Camper, 9 years old

UNCOORDINATED AT CLEANUP

Counselor (volunteer):

One of your campers is a big pain when it comes to cleanup. He's lazy and really messy. During cleanup he fools around with other campers—which makes cleanup take longer. He's always the last to finish cleaning up. When you tell him to clean up, he comes up with excuses that prevent him from making his bed or sorting his laundry. Sometimes he wanders off and disappears. It's maddening. Not only have you had enough with his behavior, but his bunkmates have lost patience with him too. Because cleanup takes so long, they are always late to activities. Lay down the law and get him to stop being so lazy.

Camper (9 years old):

You have Attention Deficit Disorder (A.D.D.), something your parents neglected to mention on your confidential. One of the downsides of having A.D.D. is that you cannot process complex tasks unless they are broken down into a list of instructions and you accomplish each step before being given the next one. You are embarrassed and don't want your bunkmates to know that you have A.D.D. You try to cover for your shortcomings by joking around during cleanup. Your counselors think you are lazy and are very frustrated with you. Even your bunkmates have had enough, because they can't go out to activity until you are done with cleanup.

First Line: "You wanted to see me?"

UNCOORDINATED AT CLEANUP

Male Camper, 9 years old

Counselor (volunteer):

One of your campers is a big pain when it comes to cleanup. He's lazy and really messy. During cleanup he fools around with other campers—which makes cleanup take longer. He's always the last to finish cleaning up. When you tell him to clean up, he comes up with excuses that prevent him from making his bed or sorting his laundry. Sometimes he wanders off and disappears. It's maddening. Not only have you had enough with his behavior, but his bunkmates have lost patience with him too. Because cleanup takes so long, they are always late to activities. Lay down the law and get him to stop being so lazy.

CAMPER HITS SOMEONE AT ACTIVITY 1ST TIME   Male Camper, 10 years old

Counselor (volunteer):

You watch one of your 10-year-old campers drop his tennis racquet, which accidentally falls on another kid's foot. You are shocked to see this other kid punch him in the face for being so careless. You send a counselor to call the Health Center for some ice, and you pull the camper aside to find out why he hit him. There is a no hitting rule at camp. Map out consequences.

First Line: *"Why did you just punch someone in the face?"*

Camper (10 years old):

You are at tennis and someone accidentally drops his racquet on your foot. Without thinking you punch him in the face. He cries, someone calls the Health Center for ice, and you get in trouble. If the counselor asks you why you did it, just tell him you didn't mean to, it was just a reflex. You have seen other kids hit in the group. Counselor speaks first.

CAMPER HITS SOMEONE AT ACTIVITY 1ST TIME   Male Camper, 10 years old

Counselor (volunteer):

You watch one of your 10-year-old campers drop his tennis racquet, which accidentally falls on another kid's foot. You are shocked to see this other kid punch him in the face for being so careless. You send a counselor to call the Health Center for some ice, and you pull the camper aside to find out why he hit him. There is a no hitting rule at camp. Map out consequences.

First Line: *"Why did you just punch someone in the face?"*

CAMPER HITS SOMEONE AT ACTIVITY 2ND TIME   Male Camper, 10 years old

Counselor (volunteer):

You listen to a fight escalate in the bunk. One of your 10-year-old campers, who got in trouble earlier today for hitting, has just hit another kid for refusing to turn down his music. Deal with the situation.

First Line: "Did you just hit him?"

Camper (10 years old):

You are in the bunk hanging out during Rest Hour and one of your bunkmates refuses to lower his music, which is playing (in your opinion) way too loud. You ask nicely twice, and when he still refuses, you punch him in the arm and demand that he turn it down. A counselor, who was reading on his bed, asks to talk to you.

Second Line: "Yes, but in my defense, I did ask him nicely—twice!—and he refused?"

CAMPER HITS SOMEONE AT ACTIVITY 2ND TIME   Male Camper, 10 years old

Counselor (volunteer):

You listen to a fight escalate in the bunk. One of your 10-year-old campers, who got in trouble earlier today for hitting, has just hit another kid for refusing to turn down his music. Deal with the situation.

First Line: "Did you just hit him?"

CAMPER HITS SOMEONE AT ACTIVITY 3RD TIME Male Camper, 10 years old

Counselor (volunteer):

During a basketball game, a camper, who has gotten in trouble twice before for hitting, gets into a shouting match with another player and before you know it a shoving match ensues. You can't believe your eyes. This is the third time you are talking to him about the same issue! Your co-counselor takes the other camper aside to talk to him, while you talk to your repeat offender.

Camper (10 years old):

During a basketball game, you accuse someone of cheating. Your shouting match quickly turns physical. You didn't shove him first, but you did shove back. Your counselor wants to talk to you.

First Line: "He pushed me first!"

CAMPER HITS SOMEONE AT ACTIVITY 3RD TIME   Male Camper, 10 years old

Counselor (volunteer):

During a basketball game, a camper, who has gotten in trouble twice before for hitting, gets into a shouting match with another player and before you know it a shoving match ensues. You can't believe your eyes. This is the third time you are talking to him about the same issue! Your co-counselor takes the other camper aside to talk to him, while you talk to your repeat offender.

CAMPER HITS SOMEONE AT ACTIVITY 5TH TIME   Male Camper, 10 years old

Counselor (volunteer):

You have absolutely had it! One of your campers has hit someone again! He's gotten into fights every day for five days in a row. This time it was because someone was annoying him. You are at your wits end. Figure out a way to deal with him.

Camper (10 years old):

You realize now that you you have an anger management issue. You can't help yourself. Whenever you find yourself in situations where you are frustrated or feel threatened, your response is to use brute force. It's not even premeditated. It just happens. You have gotten in trouble for hitting for the fifth time. This time was because someone was annoying you. Say whatever you need to so you don't get sent home.

First Line: "It wasn't my fault. He kept taunting and taunting me. He did it just to get me in trouble."

CAMPER HITS SOMEONE AT ACTIVITY 5TH TIME   Male Camper, 10 years old

Counselor (volunteer):

You have absolutely had it! One of your campers has hit someone again! He's gotten into fights every day for five days in a row. This time it was because someone was annoying him. You are at your wits end. Figure out a way to deal with him.

Male Camper, 10 years old

SCARY STORY

Counselor (volunteer):

One of your campers is constantly getting into fights. You've already talked to him about using words to resolve conflict, that hitting is not allowed at camp, and that if it happens again there are going to be some consequences. His bunkmates had a group meeting without him, and voted that they want him sent home. Talk to him.

Camper (10 years old):

While on an overnight, one of your counselors told a really scary story freaked you out. Four years ago your grandmother died and since then you've been suffering from night terrors. Your parents didn't mention it on your confidential, because they didn't want anyone making fun of you. Now you have trouble going to sleep at night and are getting cranky during the day, which has resulted in you getting into some arguments and fights with your bunkmates. You haven't said anything about being scared, because you don't want to seem like a wimp to your friends.

First Line: **"You wanted to see me?"**

SCARY STORY

Male Camper, 10 years old

Counselor (volunteer):

One of your campers is constantly getting into fights. You've already talked to him about using words to resolve conflict, that hitting is not allowed at camp, and that if it happens again there are going to be some consequences. His bunkmates had a group meeting without him, and voted that they want him sent home. Talk to him.

Male Camper, 10 years old

TEASING

Counselor (volunteer):

You walk into the bunk and witness one of your campers punch another camper in the chest. Handle the situation.

Camper 1 (10 years old):

You hit Camper 2, because he keeps teasing you and making fun of what you are wearing or how you talk or what you like to do. Several times you asked him to stop, and he wouldn't so you punched him in the arm. That seemed to work. He's not teasing you anymore. But he is crying.

First Line: [carefully mime punching Camper 2 in the arm.]

Camper 2 (10 years old):

People are just WAY too sensitive. They can't take a joke. I mean come on. Isn't this camp? What's a little light-hearted teasing among friends? You see your counselors teasing each other. You don't understand why you are in trouble. They should be talking to your friend about not being such a crybaby. I mean suck it up. If he can't handle a little teasing, maybe he should go to Girls' Side.

Second Line: "OW! Hey, what did you do that for????"

TEASING

Male Camper, 10 years old

Counselor (volunteer):

You walk into the bunk and witness one of your campers punch another camper in the chest.

Handle the situation.

WON'T TRY NEW THINGS

Male Camper, 10 years old

Counselor (volunteer):

To shake things up you decided to schedule England Day—and spend the day playing games and sports from England. The first game of the day was cricket, which was spoiled because one of your campers refused to play. Soccer was also a bust, because you had the exact number of campers to play, but again this camper (10 years old) refused to play. The kids are getting frustrated with him. Now you are about to play rugby, and he—once again—refuses to play. You get the impression that he is a spoiled kid and always gets his way at home. The group is about to riot if this kid gets his way again and spoils another activity. Talk to him.

Camper (10 years old):

You are a kid with very low self-esteem. In the past your parents have put a lot of pressure on you to be perfect, so you don't like to be in situations where you can fail. As a result you don't like to try new things. Especially sports or activities that require coordination. Your division is about to play rugby and they are all waiting for you to join them. You request to sit out.

First Line: "*I don't really feel like playing this game either. I'm going to sit this one out.*"

WON'T TRY NEW THINGS

Male Camper, 10 years old

Counselor (volunteer):

To shake things up you decided to schedule England Day—and spend the day playing games and sports from England. The first game of the day was cricket, which was spoiled because one of your campers refused to play. Soccer was also a bust, because you had the exact number of campers to play, but again this camper (10 years old) refused to play. The kids are getting frustrated with him. Now you are about to play rugby, and he—once again—refuses to play. You get the impression that he is a spoiled kid and always gets his way at home. The group is about to riot if this kid gets his way again and spoils another activity. Talk to him.

2 Campers (1 Male, 1 Female), 11 years old

BLOW OUT

Counselor (volunteer):

During a coed bowling Social you hear a commotion on another lane. When you go over there you discover a male camper drenched in soda and a female camper holding an empty pitcher. He is furious and demands that you, as the counselor, make her apologize. Handle the situation.

Male Camper (11 years old):

While bowling with your friends at a bowling Social your camp girlfriend's bunkmate comes up to you and tells you that she is dumping you. You are annoyed that she didn't have the courage to tell you herself, so you go up to your girlfriend and call her a "coward" and a "bitch" which, for some reason, makes her angry. She dumps a pitcher of soda over your head. All of her friends laugh at you. You storm off to her counselor and demand that she makes her camper apologize for being an "obnoxious bitch."

Female Camper (11 years old):

At a bowling Social you decided to send a friend to break up with your boyfriend. She delivers the news to him and for some reason he angrily marches over to your lane and calls you a "coward" and a "bitch" in front of your friends! You promptly take a pitcher of soda and pour it over his head. He then storms off to tell on you.

Female Camper First Line: I don't know what the big deal is. I was only fooling around.

BLOW OUT

2 Campers (1 Male, 1 Female), 11 years old

Counselor (volunteer):

During a coed bowling Social you hear a commotion on another lane. When you go over there you discover a male camper drenched in soda and a female camper holding an empty pitcher. He is furious and demands that you, as the counselor, make her apologize. Handle the situation.

Male Camper, 11 years old

WON'T DO AN ACTIVITY—2

Counselor (volunteer):

An overweight camper in your group (11 years old) never wants to do soccer. Every time soccer is scheduled, it is a battle to get him to join in the activity. Convince him to do the activity.

Camper (11 years old):

Every time you do sports you end up on the "skins." Sometimes your bunkmates tease you at how pale your skin is. You are embarrassed about your weight and don't feel comfortable running around with your shirt off. Make whatever excuse you can to get out of playing.

First Line: "I'm not doing soccer. I don't feel well."

WON'T DO AN ACTIVITY—2

Counselor (volunteer):

An overweight camper in your group (11 years old) never wants to do soccer. Every time soccer is scheduled, it is a battle to get him to join in the activity. Convince him to do the activity.

Male Camper, 11 years old

Male Camper, 12 years old

HAZING

Group Leader (volunteer):

One of your new campers (12 years old) is always tattling on others. You don't mind if your campers tell you about important issues, but every day it's the same annoying routine of him telling you his serious complaints: "So-and-so took an extra chocolate milk, what's-his-name borrowed my tennis racquet without asking, yadayada keeps hitting another kid, no one used sunscreen today, etc." Today he is whining that one of his bunkmates took a picture of him. Enough already! For your sanity and for the sanity of the group, talk to him about his endless "serious complaints."

Camper (12 years old):

This is your first summer at camp, and because you are so nervous you have been perhaps a little chatty. You are one of those people who see the value in rules and follow them. You don't think it's fair if people break rules without consequences. So if someone breaks a rule you do what you have been instructed to do—tell a counselor. A lot of rules get broken, so you have been reporting A LOT OF incidents to your counselor. Your bunkmates are getting annoyed that you have been "ratting them out." They told you all new kids have to be initiated into the group, which entails taking a 30 second ice-cold shower. When you are getting out of the shower, they take a picture of you. You demand they delete it, but they won't. None of your counselors will listen to yet another complaint from you, so you talk to your Group Leader about the hazing.

First Line: "Oh there you are. I have a serious complaint."

HAZING

Group Leader (volunteer):

Male Camper, 12 years old

One of your new campers (12 years old) is always tattling on others. You don't mind if your campers tell you about important issues, but everyday it's the same annoying routine of him telling you his serious complaints: "So-and-so took an extra chocolate milk, what's-his-name borrowed my tennis racquet without asking, yadayada keeps hitting another kid, no one used sunscreen today, etc." Today he is whining that one of his bunkmates took a picture of him. Enough already! For your sanity and for the sanity of the group, talk to him about his endless "serious complaints."

Male Camper, 12 years old

SLAP HAPPY

Counselor (volunteer):

This one particular camper has gotten into fight after fight. He is the kind of camper who when teased, teases back. He never backs down from a challenge, and consequently, he always gets into fights. You saw this particular incident on the tennis court. The other camper was unaware that someone was standing behind him, when he swung his racquet. The incident was an accident, pure and simple. The other camper (as usual) over-reacted.

Camper (12 years old):

During a tennis practice someone swings a racquet and hits you in the arm. You respond by hitting him over the head with your racquet. A fight breaks out and you get into trouble. You get into fights all the time, but you are stunned that you are the one who has gotten in trouble, when clearly the other person started the fight by hitting you first. You don't have any friends at home, because you get into fights easily as well.

First Line: *"He hit me on purpose! Why isn't he in trouble?"*

SLAP HAPPY

Male Camper, 12 years old

Counselor (volunteer):

This one particular camper has gotten into fight after fight after fight. He is the kind of camper who when teased, teases back. He never backs down from a challenge, and consequently, he always gets into fights. You saw this particular incident on the tennis court. The other camper was unaware that someone was standing behind him, when he swung his racquet. The incident was an accident, pure and simple. The other camper (as usual) over-reacted.

Male Camper, 12 years old

SUPER COMPETITIVE

Counselor (volunteer):

During a basketball tournament you notice your point guard is hogging the ball and not passing it around. He's taking all the shots. Even though he is making all his baskets, that's not the way you want to win the game. You prefer teamwork. You've called a timeout. See if you can convince him to be more of a team player.

Camper (12 years old):

Your goal during this basketball tournament was to break the camp's single-game scoring record. Even though other people are open for shots, you don't pass to them. Your teammates are getting frustrated with you. You feel they are being petty. Your team is winning because of your competitive edge. Your Coach calls a time out to talk to you. Don't let him get in the way of breaking the camp record.

First Line: "Aren't I doing awesome? I rock!!"

SUPER COMPETITIVE

Male Camper, 12 years old

Counselor (volunteer):

During a basketball tournament you notice your point guard is hogging the ball and not passing it around. He's taking all the shots. Even though he is making all his baskets, that's not the way you want to win the game. You prefer teamwork. You've called a timeout. See if you can convince him to be more of a team player.

TEASER AND BYSTANDER

Counselor (volunteer):

You are about to enter a bunk when you hear trouble brewing inside. Two kids appear to be teasing one of their bunkmates relentlessly about a rash cream he has to put on his bottom. On closer listening, only one of them is doing the actual teasing, the other one says nothing except laughs as his friend torments the other kid. He keeps yelling for the Teaser to stop tormenting him, but his pleas are unsuccessful. Before this turns into an all out fight, you poke your head in the bunk and ask to talk to the Teaser and the Bystander outside on the porch.

Teaser and Bystander (12 years old):

One of your bunkmates has impetigo (a contagious skin rash) and has to rub a medicated cream all over his ass. You think this is hilarious, because this is the kid who never shares any of his candy or lets anyone play with any of his games. And now he has a nasty rash. You (Teaser) decide to make his life miserable and crack humiliating jokes while your friend (Bystander) just points and laughs. Just as it's getting really good, your counselor interrupts your fun. Defend your position that you (Teaser) were only giving this kid what he deserved. Bystander, your defense is that you shouldn't get in trouble, because you weren't doing anything.

Teaser's First Line: "*Oh come on! Just when it was getting good!!*"
Bystander's First Line: "*Why am I in trouble? I didn't say anything.*"

2 Male Campers, 12 years old

TEASER AND BYSTANDER

2 Male Campers, 12 years old

Counselor (volunteer):

You are about to enter a bunk when you hear trouble brewing inside. Two kids appear to be teasing one of their bunkmates relentlessly about a rash cream he has to put on his bottom. On closer listening, only one of them is doing the actual teasing, the other one says nothing except laughs as his friend torments the other kid. He keeps yelling for the Teaser to stop tormenting him, but his pleas are unsuccessful. Before this turns into an all out fight, you poke your head in the bunk and ask to talk to the Teaser and the Bystander outside on the porch.

INAPPROPRIATE DIGITAL PHOTOS

Counselor (volunteer):

You walk into a bunk and discover one of your campers is taking shots of his new digital camera. He is photographing them mooning the camera and streaking around naked. They are not being coerced; they all appear to be doing so willingly. Handle the situation.

Camper (12 years old):

You are taking some funny shots of your bunkmates (streaking around and mooning, etc.) with your new digital camera to post on your Facebook account when you get home. The fun is interrupted when your counselor walks in. If he demands that you erase the pictures or hand in the camera, refuse to do so. You have a right to post whatever you want on Facebook. You've seen his Facebook page and have seen plenty of inappropriate pictures of him getting drunk with his friends, etc. So what's the big deal?

First Line: "Hey, you gotta check out these photos."

Male Camper, 12 years old

INAPPROPRIATE DIGITAL PHOTOS

Male Camper, 12 years old

Counselor (volunteer):

You walk into a bunk and discover one of your campers is taking shots of his bunkmates with his new digital camera. He is photographing them mooning the camera and streaking around naked. They are not being coerced; they all appear to be doing so willingly. Handle the situation.

2 Male Campers, 13 years old

CAUGHT MASTURBATING

Counselor (volunteer):

As Head OD you are getting lights out on the Lower Hill, when you hear a commotion from one of the Upper Hill bunks. You listen at the screen door before entering and hear everyone laughing hilariously about something. You also hear someone in the bathroom crying. You enter the bunk.

First Line: *"What's going on guys?"*

Camper 1 (13 years old):

It is after Taps and you were in bed under your covers discreetly masturbating, when one of your bunkmates noticed, pulled off the covers and started making fun of you. You are humiliated and run into the bathroom to hide. He continues to make "jerk-off" comments and jokes about the size of your penis. You beg him to stop. He refuses.

Camper 2 (13 years old):

You were hanging out with your friends in the bunk. It's five more minutes to lights out, when you notice one of your bunkmates is doing something odd under the covers. Your friends goad you to sneak over and rip off the covers. You discover him in the midst of masturbating. Everyone laughs except him of course. He runs into the bathroom. Encouraged by your friend's laughter you continue to make light of the situation. In your mind, you are just trying to defuse the situation and make him see the absurdity.

CAUGHT MASTURBATING

2 Male Campers, 13 years old

Counselor (volunteer):

As Head OD you are getting lights out on the Lower Hill, when you hear a commotion from one of the Upper Hill bunks. You listen at the screen door before entering and hear everyone laughing hilariously about something. You also hear someone in the bathroom crying. You enter the bunk.

First Line: "What's going on guys?"

COMPARING PENIS SIZES

Male Camper, 13 years old

Counselor (volunteer):

You walk into the bunk to discover one of your campers (13 years old) has organized his ten bunkmates to have a contest while they wait for the shower to get hot. You discover them lying naked on their beds, giggling and comparing boner sizes. When you walk into the bunk, some get embarrassed and duck under the covers, but everyone else just thinks it's funny. Ask to talk to the person who organized the contest. Talk to him about appropriate behavior at camp.

Camper (13 years old):

You and your bunkmates are waiting to shower and are lying on your beds and you organize a contest to see who has the largest boner. Right in the middle of the contest, your counselor walks in and asks what's going on. Tell him he's just in time. He doesn't think it's funny. He asks you to get dressed and meet him on the porch to talk to him. You're 13, it's camp, and you can't imagine what his problem is. Besides you've heard that when he was a camper he did worse!

First Line: "You wanted to see me?"

COMPARING PENIS SIZES

Male Camper, 13 years old

Counselor (volunteer):

You walk into the bunk to discover one of your campers (13 years old) has organized his ten bunkmates to have a contest while they wait for the shower to get hot. You discover them lying naked on their beds, giggling and comparing boner sizes. When you walk into the bunk, some get embarrassed and duck under the covers, but everyone else just thinks it's funny. Ask to talk to the person who organized the contest. Talk to him about appropriate behavior at camp.

Male Camper, 14 years old

STEALING CANDY

Counselor (volunteer):

You are about to walk into your bunk when you observe an Upper Hill camper (14 years old) stealing candy from one of your kid's care packages. You confront him. By the way, other items have recently disappeared (CDs, game cartridges, a tennis racquet etc.) and you suspect this camper may be behind these thefts as well. Mention this to him. He might be the culprit behind your division's crime wave—don't let him off easily.

First Line: "What are you doing in here?"

Camper (14 years old):

You are caught stealing candy from a Lower Hill bunk. Weasel your way out of it. Deny it. Say you had permission. Say people stole your candy when you were a lower hill camper, so what's the big deal? It's not like you stole a CD, it's only candy. [Important: You have only stolen candy—nothing else.] Also, you've seen counselors in the bunk steal candy from their own campers. Counselor has first line.

STEALING CANDY

Male Camper, 14 years old

Counselor (volunteer):

You are about to walk into your bunk when you observe an Upper Hill camper (14 years old) stealing candy from one of your kid's care packages. You confront him. By the way, other items have recently disappeared (CDs, game cartridges, a tennis racquet etc.) and you suspect this camper may be behind these thefts as well. Mention this to him. He might be the culprit behind your division's crime wave—don't let him off easily.

First Line: "What are you doing in here?"

192

CAMPER BLACK MARKETEER

Counselor (volunteer):

You get wind that one of your campers (14 years old) has been selling items from his care packages at exorbitant prices to the younger campers. Now they have no money for their upcoming trip. They ask you to get their money back for them.

Camper (14 years old):

Your parents have been sending you care packages weekly. You notice that some of the younger campers aren't getting any packages. You don't think it's fair that they have nothing while you have plenty. So you decide to make items in your care packages available to them...for a price. Your price scheme includes selling cans of soda for $5, Pringles for $10, $2 for candy bars.... One of the Sophomores (9 years old) even traded his iPod for a case of Cup O' Noodles. In addition to the iPod you have made $125. Your counselor wants to speak to you about your little "Black Market." Assume he is coming as a consumer and offer him discounts on some of your popular items. If he tries to make you return the money, tell him you earned it fair and square.

First Line: "Are you here to buy some snacks?."

Male Camper, 14 years old

CAMPER BLACK MARKETEER

Male Camper, 14 years old

Counselor (volunteer):

You get wind that one of your campers (14 years old) has been selling items from his care packages at exorbitant prices to the younger campers. Now they have no money for their upcoming trip.

They ask you to get their money back for them.

LAST IN GROUP TO REACH PUBERTY

Male Camper, 15 years old

Counselor (volunteer):

You are hanging out listening to some music in the bunk while your 15-year-old campers are showering for a Social. One of your campers comes over, says he has something on his mind, and asks if he can ask you a couple of questions. Try to help him out.

Camper (15 years old):

Everyone in your division has gone through puberty except for you. This has left you frustrated and confused. While hanging out with your counselor ask him some questions that you have been curious about: "Is it normal to masturbate? etc." Insist on him telling you. Everyone else has gone through puberty so they already know. You are tired of being left out of the conversations.

First Line: *"Can I ask you a question in private? Is it normal to masturbate?"*

LAST IN GROUP TO REACH PUBERTY

Male Camper, 15 years old

Counselor (volunteer):

You are hanging out listening to some music in the bunk while your 15-year-old campers are showering for a Social. One of your campers comes over, says he has something on his mind, and asks if he can ask you a couple of questions. Try to help him out.

Male Camper, 15 years old

THE INTIMIDATOR

Counselor (volunteer):

You have noticed one of your campers (15 years old) has been intimidating his bunkmates in order to get his way. For some reason they are letting him get away with it. You ask to speak with him so you can put a stop to this. Try to get him to the point where he will apologize to his bunkmates and make amends.

Camper (15 years old):

You are physically the biggest camper in the division and a leader. All of the campers look up to you. Like some of your counselors, you take advantage of the perks of leadership. If someone won't do your chores during cleanup, you stare them down. If someone won't let you be first in line at the Mess Hall, you just ignore them and step ahead of them. Now your counselor wants to talk to you about your behavior. If he threatens to punish you, tell him that you don't know what he is talking about. You haven't laid a hand on anyone.

First Line: **"You wanted to see me?"**

THE INTIMIDATOR

Male Camper, 15 years old

Counselor (volunteer):

You have noticed one of your campers (15 years old) has been intimidating his bunkmates in order to get his way. For some reason they are letting him get away with it. You ask to speak with him so you can put a stop to this. Try to get him to the point where he will apologize to his bunkmates and make amends.

Camper-Counselor Conflicts

Male Camper, 10 years old

ALWAYS LAST

Counselor (volunteer):

One of your 10-year-old campers appears to have A.D.D. At most activities he is a space cadet—never truly engaged. At his favorite activity, he is super focused and active. Be that as it may, walking to meals or activities he is always last. His bunkmates are getting really impatient with him and think he is doing it on purpose. Motivate him to get to activities faster so that you can keep your group on schedule and can keep peace in your group.

Camper (10 years old):

There is one saying that your grandmother told you that really made an impression on you: "Stop and smell the roses." She said your grandfather never did it. When he was alive, he never took the time to enjoy the simpler things, and missed out on a lot of sunsets, smiles, birthdays, etc. You've decided you don't want that to be your life, so you take your time and never rush through your day. You take in the sky, the breeze, the people passing by. People are more important to you than schedules, and because you don't know how long you or they will be on this Earth you seize the moment! Unfortunately, your counselor doesn't share your devil-may-care pace through the day and wants to talk to you. Maybe it's time you share your point of view with your counselor and convince him that he should bend to your way of life.

First Line: "You wanted to see me?"

ALWAYS LAST

Male Camper, 10 years old

Counselor (volunteer):

One of your 10-year-old campers appears to have A.D.D. At most activities he is a space cadet—never truly engaged. At his favorite activity, he is super focused and active. Be that as it may, walking to meals or activities he is always last. His bunkmates are getting tired of waiting for him, and other counselors are getting really impatient with him and think he is doing it on purpose. Motivate him to get to activities faster so that you can keep your group on schedule and can keep peace in your group.

CAMPER GETS A HOOK THROUGH HIS LIP

Male Camper, 10 years old

Counselor (volunteer):

You are fishing with your campers on an overnight off camp grounds. You are using a pair of wire cutters to cut a tangled line, when you hear a commotion behind you. Even though you strictly forbid anyone from casting, someone has, and they caught their hook through someone's lip. There are no doctors or nurses on your trip. Deal with the crisis at hand.

Camper (10 years old):

You are on an overnight with your group fishing on a dock, using drop lines. Unfortunately, someone decides to ignore the "no casting" rule and in the attempt to do so, causes his hook to go through your lip. You are off camp, so there are no doctors or nurses nearby.

First Line: **"Ow! His hook went through my lip!"**

CAMPER GETS A HOOK THROUGH HIS LIP

Male Camper, 10 years old

Counselor (volunteer):

You are fishing with your campers on an overnight off camp grounds. You are using a pair of wire cutters to cut a tangled line, when you hear a commotion behind you. Even though you strictly forbid anyone from casting, someone has, and they caught their hook through someone's lip. There are no doctors or nurses on your trip. Deal with the crisis at hand.

Male Camper, 10 years old

MONEY IN YOUR WALLET IS MISSING

Counselor (volunteer):

No one wanted to sleep by the door because the spring on the screen door makes it slam pretty loud, so you took it. You normally hide your wallet under some towels on your shelf by the door. Several times you have come back to your bunk to discover your towels in a mess on your bed with your wallet half open on top of them. You can't be sure, but you think there is some money missing from your wallet. The camper who sleeps next to you is the only one who has borrowed towels from you in the past. He previously has complained of never having any money, and now all of a sudden he has $5. Confront him. Ask him why your wallet is out in the open and why he all of a sudden has money. You've caught him lying in the past. Find out if he is lying and ask him to return the money.

Camper (10 years old):

You sleep next to a counselor whose bed is by the door. Once in a while you borrow a towel from him. He doesn't seem to mind to occasionally do you a favor. You do him favors too. He doesn't realize it, because he is not always around, but the banging of the screen door often knocks towels off his shelf and you put them back on the shelf for him. On this occasion, just as you are about to put his wallet and towels back on the shelf he comes in and accuses you of messing with his stuff and taking money from your wallet. He even thinks the $5 you got from your grandmother is from his wallet. You've been caught lying before, but you are not lying now.

First Line: **"Your towels fell; I was just putting them back."**

MONEY IN YOUR WALLET IS MISSING

Male Camper, 10 years old

Counselor (volunteer):

No one wanted to sleep by the door because the spring on the screen door makes it slam pretty loud, so you took it. You normally hide your wallet under some towels on your shelf by the door. Several times you have come back to your bunk to discover your towels in a mess on your bed with your wallet half open on top of them. You can't be sure, but you think there is some money missing from your wallet. The camper who sleeps next to you is the only one who has borrowed towels from you in the past. He previously has complained of never having any money, and now all of a sudden he has $5. Confront him. Ask him why your wallet is out in the open and why he all of a sudden has money. You've caught him lying in the past. Find out if he is lying and ask him to return the money.

Male Camper, 10 years old

CUT FROM TEAM

Counselor (volunteer):

You notice a camper (ten years old) check the newly posted roster for a tournament team (that you are coaching) and then walk away pissed. You go over to the camper to talk to him. Let him know that he worked real hard and that there is always next year.

Camper (10 years old):

You have just checked the bulletin board and for the third year in a row you have discovered that you didn't make the big tournament team. You feel upset because the counselor coaching the team always picks his favorites. You feel you are as good or better than the others who made the team and that the counselor is being unfair. Hearing the phrases, "You worked hard, but try again next year," or "there'll be other tournaments" make you even angrier.

First Line: "Camp sucks."

CUT FROM TEAM

Male Camper, 10 years old

Counselor (volunteer):

You notice a camper (ten years old) check the newly posted roster for a tournament team (that you are coaching) and then walk away pissed. You go over to the camper to talk to him. Let him know that he worked real hard and that there is always next year.

Male Camper, 11 years old

BOUNCING OFF THE WALLS

Counselor (volunteer):

You are OD for a group of very rambunctious 11-year-olds. The group is led by one camper, who has single-handedly turned your quiet night into a hellish nightmare. He has incited his bunkmates to: play Ultimate Frisbee in the bunk, have pillow fights, wrestle, raid other bunks… It is past lights out and they are still bouncing off the walls. The Head OD has twice asked you to get your kids quieted down and the lights out. You feel you are losing control of the group. The ringleader has asked to speak with you.

Camper (11 years old):

You are so pumped to be at camp that you are bouncing off the walls. You organize a game of Frisbee in the bunk, but—fearful that a window is going to get broken—your counselors make you stop. You then organize a pillow fight in the bunk. When your counselors make you stop that, you decide to raid another bunk. The counselors won't let you do anything fun!

First Line: **"This camp sucks! You never let us do anything fun."**

BOUNCING OFF THE WALLS

Male Camper, 11 years old

Counselor (volunteer):

You are OD for a group of very rambunctious 11-year-olds. The group is led by one camper, who has single handedly turned your quiet night into a hellish nightmare. He has incited his bunkmates to: play Ultimate Frisbee in the bunk, have pillow fights, wrestle, raid other bunks… It is past lights out and they are still bouncing off the walls. The Head OD has twice asked you to get your kids quieted down and the lights out. You feel you are losing control of the group. The ringleader has asked to speak with you.

Male Camper, 11 years old

LOST AND FOUND CHAMP

Counselor (volunteer):

Every day the Head of Waterfront and the Head Counselor give you a pile of clothes belonging to one of your campers. He leaves behind clothes, equipment, and personal belongings. He is always losing things. What's worse, he is now borrowing from his bunkmates, and losing those things too. It wouldn't be so bad, if he didn't change 3 or 4 times a day! His bed area is always a mess, and you are at your wits end how to make your summer not be all about picking up after this kid. Talk to him at your first opportunity.

Camper (11 years old):

Even though you came to camp with a ton of clothes you never seem to have enough clean clothes to last you until the next laundry day. You go through three changes of clothes a day, plus somehow your clothes just disappear. You have no idea what happens to them. You ask your counselor to call home to ask your parents to send you more sneakers, socks, t-shirts, shorts, and sweatshirts. Oh, also another baseball glove, tennis racquet, and iPod. And one more flip flop. Not a pair. You have the left one; you just need the right one.

First Line: "Can I call home?"

LOST AND FOUND CHAMP

Male Camper, 11 years old

Counselor (volunteer):

Every day the Head of Waterfront and the Head Counselor give you a pile of clothes belonging to one of your campers. He leaves behind clothes, equipment, and personal belongings. He is always losing things. What's worse, he is now borrowing from his bunkmates, and losing those things too. It wouldn't be so bad, if he didn't change 3 or 4 times a day! His bed area is always a mess, and you are at your wits end how to make your summer not be all about picking up after this kid. Talk to him at your first opportunity.

Male Camper, 11 years old

REFUSES TO LEAVE THE SOCIAL

Counselor (volunteer):

You are at the big DJ Dance Party with your division of 11-year-olds. To make room for everyone at the Social Hall, they've staggered the arrivals and departures of the groups. The Lower Hill campers (like yours) arrive earlier, but also leave earlier. One of your campers, has made himself scarce, when they've announced that it was time for the group to go. The whole group waits with another counselor while you go back and find him. When you finally find him he refuses to leave. He wants to stay to the end. His bunkmates are tired of him thinking rules don't apply to him, and your co-counselor is getting stressed trying to keep the group from wandering off. Handle the situation.

Camper (11 years old):

You are having a great time at the DJ Dance Party and it's time for your group to go back. You want to hang out with your older brother and make it really hard for your counselors to find you. When one of your counselors does find you, you dig in your heels and absolutely refuse to go back. It's absolutely unfair that, just because you are a year younger than the kids on the Upper Hill, that you have to have a shorter night. Your whole group is waiting for you, so that you can all return to your bunks with your OD. Make your counselor come up with a convincing reason why you can't return to your bunk, when your older brother returns to his an hour or two later.

First Line: *"Don't waste your time. I'm not going and you can't make me!"*

REFUSES TO LEAVE THE SOCIAL

Male Camper, 11 years old

Counselor (volunteer):

You are at the big DJ Dance Party with your division of 11-year-olds. To make room for everyone at the Social Hall, they've staggered the arrivals and departures of the groups. The Lower Hill campers (like yours) arrive earlier, but also leave earlier. One of your campers, has made himself scarce, when they've announced that it was time for the group to go. The whole group waits with another counselor while you go back and find him. When you finally find him he refuses to leave. He wants to stay to the end. His bunkmates are tired of him thinking rules don't apply to him, and your co-counselor is getting stressed trying to keep the group from wandering off. Handle the situation.

DISRESPECTFUL TO COUNSELOR

Male Camper, 11 years old

Counselor (volunteer):

One of the things campers agree to when they come to camp is not to use foul language. Everyone in the group seems to respect this except for one of your campers (11 years old) who curses like a truck driver. You have reminded him on numerous occasions not to use that kind of language. You see the Camp Director approaching. He is giving a tour to a prospective family. In the meantime your camper is spilling forth an aria of f-bombs. You need to get him to correct his behavior now and for the future.

First Line: "Hey, you know you're not allowed to use that kind of language here at camp! Enough is enough!"

Camper (11 years old):

Back home your parents don't seem to care that you use curse words. But at camp, people go nuts if you drop the f-bomb. On this particular day, one of your bunkmates refuses to give you your iPod back, and so you let loose a string of colorful f-words, using them imaginatively as every part of speech. Your counselor comes over and tells you that if you curse one more time, that you are going to be in a lot of trouble. Who the hell is he to tell you that, so you give him the finger! This, of course, does not make him happy. Defend your right to exercise your Freedom of Speech.

[after the counselor tells you not to swear anymore, give him the finger]

DISRESPECTFUL TO COUNSELOR

Male Camper, 11 years old

Counselor (volunteer):

One of the things campers agree to when they come to camp is not to use foul language. Everyone in the group seems to respect this except for one of your campers (11 years old) who curses like a truck driver. You have reminded him on numerous occasions not to use that kind of language. You see the Camp Director approaching. He is giving a tour to a prospective family. In the meantime your camper is spilling forth an aria of F-bombs. You need to get him to correct his behavior now and for the future.

First Line: "Hey, you know you're not allowed to use that kind of language here at camp! Enough is enough!"

CAMPERS THINK THE ACTIVITIES SUCK

Male Camper, 11 years old

Counselor (volunteer):

At the start of the summer you went through the Confidentials very thoroughly and discovered most parents requested that their children try new activities and have a balance of athletic and non-athletic activities. One of your campers (11 years old) does nothing but complain about how he hates all the fun activities that you have spent hours (and sometimes days) planning. These activities are designed to accomplish all the various goals that the parents requested for their children. You find it demoralizing—after doing all this work creating and running these activities—that this kid keeps torpedoing them down. Announce that you are about to play dodgeball.

Camper (11 years old):

You came to camp to play sports. Not to do archery, and boating, and arts and crafts, and chess. Something has compelled your lame-brained counselor to ignore the fact that your group wants to just play sports and continues to schedule a mixture of athletic and non-athletic (i.e., LAME!) events for the group. You hate playing Human Stratego and Treasure Hunts and Spud not to mention going to ceramics, woodworking, and photography. Get it through your counselor's thick head that not only do the activities suck, but he sucks for suggesting them. Sports. You want sports. You don't care about what he, your parents, or the other campers want. You came to camp to play sports all day long, and demand that he starts listening to you.

First Line: *"This activity SUCKS!"*

CAMPERS THINK THE ACTIVITIES SUCK

Male Camper, 11 years old

Counselor (volunteer):

At the start of the summer you went through the Confidentials very thoroughly and discovered most parents requested that their children try new activities and have a balance of athletic and non-athletic activities. One of your campers (11 years old) does nothing but complain about how he hates all the fun activities that you have spent hours (and sometimes days) planning. These activities are designed to accomplish all the various goals that he parents requested for their children. You find it demoralizing—after doing all this work creating and running these activities—that this kid keeps torpedoing them down. Announce that you are about to play dodgeball.

Male Camper, 11 years old

INAPPROPRIATE HUMOR

Counselor (volunteer):

One of your campers is a ticking time bomb. He has absolutely no sense of boundaries or propriety. He makes jokes about people's looks, their religion, sexual preferences, physical abnormalities...etc. Nothing is sacred with him and it is really getting to be embarrassing. The big division trip is coming up next week, and you are nervous about what he will say out in public. He just found out you are from Nantucket and is about to recite a famous limerick. Stop him before he says anything embarrassing, and talk to him about his renegade sense of humor.

Camper (11 years old):

You are the funniest camper in your division. You have a lightning wit, but most of your humor is inappropriate (making fun of body type, race, religion, etc.). You don't do it with the intention of being mean, but as you always say, sometimes the funniest jokes are based in truth. Unfortunately, that's not how those being ridiculed feel. They hate being made fun of. Even the joke you made about the camp waitress having big boobs seemed to make her annoyed. Hey, not every joke will land. The key to a good joke is timing. And the key to good timing is practice, practice, practice. Just as you are about to joke about your counselor (who you just found out is from Nantucket!), you get called onto the carpet.

First Line: "*Our counselor who is from Nantucket, has a – " (thankfully, you are interrupted*

INAPPROPRIATE HUMOR

Male Camper, 11 years old

Counselor (volunteer):

One of your campers is a ticking time bomb. He has absolutely no sense of boundaries or propriety. He makes jokes about people's looks, their religion, sexual preferences, physical abnormalities…etc. Nothing is sacred with him and it is really getting to be embarrassing. The big division trip is coming up next week, and you are nervous about what he will say out in public. He just found out you are from Nantucket and is about to recite a famous limerick. Stop him before he says anything embarrassing, and talk to him about his renegade sense of humor.

220

CAMPER USES WORDS LIKE FAG AND GAY

Male Camper, 12 years old

Counselor (volunteer):

One of your campers (12 years old) has two dads, and has complained to you that one of his bunkmates is using derogatory language. When you press him, you find out the bunkmate in question calls other kids "fags" or "faggots" or describes certain activities or types of music as "gay." You thank the camper for telling you, and promise the next time you hear his bunkmate using that language, you will talk to him.

Camper (12 years old):

One of your counselors has asked to speak to you about how you choose to express yourself. Whenever an activity is lame, you say it's "so gay." If someone pisses you off, you call him a "faggot" or a "fag." Your parents told you homosexuality is wrong—even quoting you passages from the Bible. Your parents don't see anything wrong with using words like "gay" for "fag," because if anyone who is gay is offended by those words, maybe by hearing them enough times, they'll be cured of their illness or be embarrassed enough to not continue to choose that lifestyle. They've also told you that usually the people who complain about these words are secretly gay themselves. And by the way, you're not the only one who uses these words. You've heard other kids use them. And besides, no one should be offended, because, thank God, as far as you know, no one at camp is gay.

First Line: "Do we have to go to arts and crafts? It's so gay!"

CAMPER USES WORDS LIKE FAG AND GAY

Male Camper, 12 years old

Counselor (volunteer):

One of your campers (12 years old) has two dads, and has complained to you that one of his bunk-mates is using derogatory language. When you press him, you find out the bunkmate in question calls other kids "fags" or "faggots" or describes certain activities or types of music as "gay". You thank the camper for telling you, and promise the next time you hear his bunkmate using that language, you will talk to him.

Male Camper, 13 years old

POOR SPORT: CHEATER

Counselor (volunteer):

While coaching a softball game you notice one of your players cheat. During one play, he said he had his foot on the bag and he didn't. Another time he said a ball that went foul didn't touch his glove, but you saw that it did. His cheating has put you up by two runs. Between innings, you pull him over to the side. Determine what action you need to take (i.e., say nothing and give him the benefit of the doubt, give him a warning, forfeit the game…).

First Line: "*I need to talk to you.*"

Camper (13 years old):

You are playing an important intramural game. On a couple of close calls you have cheated a little to make sure that you win the game. In intramurals, you play without umpires so both calls were yours to make. You can defend them if challenged. The other team probably cheated too at some point, so what's the big deal. The long and short of it, because of your ingenuity, your team is going to win. Counselor has first line.

POOR SPORT: CHEATER

Male Camper, 13 years old

Counselor (volunteer):

While coaching a softball game you notice one of your players cheat. During one play, he said he had his foot on the bag and he didn't. Another time he said a ball that went foul didn't touch his glove, but you saw that it did. His cheating has put you up by two runs. Between innings, you pull him over to the side. Determine what action you need to take (i.e., say nothing and give him the benefit of the doubt, give him a warning, forfeit the game…).

First Line: "I need to talk to you."

BAD OD—Part 1

Male Camper, 12 years old

Counselor (Volunteer):

You are having a difficult OD evening. The bunk has been bouncing off the walls for a while now. Just as they're settling down, one camper in particular is keeping the bunk up. The lights are turned off and the camper turns them back on as you walk away. After playing this "game" with the camper the lights are out and it is finally quiet. A few minutes later you go outside to the porch to enjoy your book when you hear loud humming. You hear several campers yell, "Stop it!" You re-enter the bunk and go over to the camper to talk to him.

First Line: ***"You. Outside. Now"***

Camper (12 years old):

Camp is supposed to be fun! All this counselor does whether at activity or free play is to scold you for being "too rowdy." For instance, at archery he spent twenty minutes explaining the rules. He is so uptight about everything. You should be able to stay up as late as you want during the summer.

Second Line: ***"What the hell is your problem? Camp is supposed to be fun."***

BAD OD—Part 1

Male Camper, 12 years old

Counselor (Volunteer):

You are having a difficult OD evening. The bunk has been bouncing off the walls for a while now. Just as they're settling down, one camper in particular is keeping the bunk up. The lights are turned off and the camper turns them back on as you walk away. After playing this "game" with the camper the lights are out and it is finally quiet. A few minutes later you go outside to the porch to enjoy your book when you hear loud humming. You hear several campers yell, "Stop it!" You re-enter the bunk and go over to the camper to talk to him.

First Line: "You. Outside. Now"

Male Camper, 12 years old

BAD OD—Part 2

Counselor (volunteer):

It's the second time you've had OD for the "Bad Bunk". Once again the same camper is being rowdy and not listening to you. Tonight he has decided to bounce up and down on his bed, singing at the top of his lungs. You tell him to stop doing that before he breaks the bed.

First Line: "Yo! You're going to break the bed. I told you it's lights out, go to sleep."

Camper (12 years old):

Your counselor is really getting on your nerves now. He constantly singles you out as the only troublemaker in this bunk. Everyone is laughing and having fun as you entertain them by bouncing on the bed and singing a spoof of last year's Sing Song. Just as he nags you about the fragility of the wooden beds, the bed frame cracks and you hit your head knocking yourself unconscious. (*Lie motionless on the ground.*) Counselor speaks first.

BAD OD—Part 2

Male Camper, 12 years old

Counselor (volunteer):

It's the second time you've had OD for the "Bad Bunk". Once again the same camper is being rowdy and not listening to you. Tonight he has decided to bounce up and down on his bed, singing at the top of his lungs. You tell him to stop doing that before he breaks the bed.

First Line: "Yo! You're going to break the bed. I told you it's lights out, go to sleep."

Male Camper, 13 years old

SEARCHING FOR STOLEN CAMERA

Counselor (volunteer):

You can't find your iPod that you left on your shelf. You begin to suspect that one of your campers took it. While he is out at activity, you hang back at the bunk and search through his things. While looking for it you come across a lighter, a cell phone, and some condoms hidden in his backpack. The camper enters the bunk just as you finish searching through his stuff.

First Line: " Oh good, I'm glad you're here. I think we need to talk."

Camper (13 years old):

You forgot your tennis racquet, and when you go back to your bunk, you discover your counselor going through your stuff. He has found your hidden stash of private possessions (lighter, cell phone, condoms). You get angry and tell him he has no right to go through your personal items. Threaten to get him fired or that you will have your parents sue him. Any time he tries to talk to you about what you did wrong, respond by telling him what he did wrong. ["But you had no right to be looking through my personal belongings!" "Even if you did have a right, you have to do it with someone else in the room." "How do I know that's not your lighter and those aren't your condoms?"

Second Line: "Ok, how about we start with I'm going to get you fired? You have no right going through my stuff."

SEARCHING FOR STOLEN CAMERA   Male Camper, 13 years old

Counselor (volunteer):

You can't find your iPod that you left on your shelf. You begin to suspect that one of your campers took it. While he is out at activity, you hang back at the bunk and search through his things. While looking for it you come across a lighter, a cell phone, and some condoms hidden in his backpack. The camper enters the bunk just as you finish searching through his stuff.

First Line: " Oh good, I'm glad you're here. I think we need to talk."

POOR SPORTSMANSHIP

Male Camper, 13 years old

Counselor (volunteer):

You've warned your division's best athlete numerous times about poor sportsmanship. Twice he's thrown a bat (not by accident) and he has also cursed out the ump. After the second bat-throwing, you warn him that if he does it again, you will throw him out of the game. He proceeds to give you the finger. You pull him aside....

First Line: "You've been warned. Come over here so I can talk to you."

Camper (13 years old):

You are the Team Captain and the best player on the field. Your baseball team is getting slaughtered, because your teammates are making stupid mistakes and your coaches are doing nothing to pull the team together. Twice you've thrown your bat after popping up. When your counselor reprimands you about poor sportsmanship, give him the finger.

POOR SPORTSMANSHIP

Male Camper, 13 years old

Counselor (volunteer):

You've warned your division's best athlete numerous times about poor sportsmanship. Twice he's thrown a bat (not by accident) and he has also cursed out the ump. After the second bat-throwing, you warn him that if he does it again, you will throw him out of the game. He proceeds to give you the finger. You pull him aside....

First Line: "You've been warned. Come over here so I can talk to you."

Male Camper, 13 years old

PORN

Counselor (volunteer):

You walk into the bunk and see a camper looking at porn on his iPod.

Camper (13 years old):

You are sitting in your bunk checking out porn on your iPod, when one of your counselors walks in on you. If he makes a big deal of it, mention that it's all good, because one of the other counselors in the division gave it to you.

First Line: "Hey check out her rack!!!"

PORN

Male Camper, 13 years old

Counselor (volunteer):
You walk into the bunk and see a camper looking at porn on his iPod.

Male Camper, 14 years old

"I DON'T HAVE TO LISTEN TO YOU"

Counselor (volunteer):

One of your 14-year-old campers is feeling his oats and mouthing off to you all the time. You don't mind him disagreeing with you or challenging your opinion. It's how he does it—in front of the whole group and using disrespectful language. You feel you have done nothing to warrant this. How could he not like you? You are hardly ever around to do anything to him to piss him off. You are tired of him being disrespectful, and have asked to speak with him.

Camper (14 years old):

Your counselor has done little to nothing to earn your respect for him. He never hangs out with your division, and when he does, he yells all the time. When he asks you to do cleanup or quiet down, you are disrespectful and mouth off to him. For you, respect is never assumed; it's earned. And until then, your counselor can just "go screw himself." You may have gone too far, because now he has asked to speak with you.

First Line: **"Make this quick, jackass, because I don't have all day."**

"I DON'T HAVE TO LISTEN TO YOU"

Counselor (volunteer):

One of your 14-year-old campers is feeling his oats and mouthing off to you all the time. You don't mind him disagreeing with you or challenging your opinion. It's how he does it—in front of the whole group and using disrespectful language. You feel you have done nothing to warrant this. How could he not like you. You are hardly ever around to do anything to him to piss him off. You are tired of him being disrespectful, and have asked to speak with him.

Male Camper, 14 years old

CAMPERS HATE THEIR COUNSELOR

Male Camper, 14 years old

Counselor (volunteer):

One of your campers has asked to speak with you about a serious issue with a counselor in your division. Ask them what's going on? After hearing the list of grievances, ask him who it is so you can speak to them.

First Line: "I heard you wanted to speak to me about one of our counselors. What's up?"

Camper (14 years old):

You are speaking on behalf of your bunk. You hate one of your counselors. During the day he never hangs out with the division, often opting to hang out with other groups or with his friends. At the end of the day he can't get out of their fast enough. When he isn't sleeping and does decide to do activities, he is sarcastic or short tempered. He screams throughout cleanup, but never offers to help or clean up himself. The activities he chooses are lame, and he never listens to feedback. He just yells. He isn't fun to be with. You'd like to see if he can be switched to another division. When the Counselor asks who it is, tell him who—Him! Make sure your Counselor comes up with a game plan to handle the situation. Counselor speaks first.

CAMPERS HATE THEIR COUNSELOR

Male Camper, 14 years old

Counselor (volunteer):

One of your campers has asked to speak with you about a serious issue with a counselor in your division. Ask them what's going on? After hearing the list of grievances, ask him who it is so you can speak to them.

First Line: "I heard you wanted to speak to me about one of our counselors. What's up?"

LAZY CAMPERS (BUNK MEETING)

3 or 4 Male Campers, 14 years old

Counselor (volunteer):

Every cleanup is a struggle. Nobody participates. The floor hasn't been swept; there is an ant problem because of wrappers and food on the floor; the trash is overflowing; wet towels and bathing suits hang from the rafters covered in flies; none of the beds are made; and there are dirty clothes everywhere. First activity is about to blow and it's their favorite activity. Motivate them to clean up.

First Line: "Guys, let's getting going on cleanup. First activity is in five minutes."

3 or 4 Campers (14 years old):

Your counselor keeps nagging you and your bunkmates to clean up. You don't see why it's a big deal. This is summer camp and not school or home. Only the counselor seems to care that the bunk is a mess. You're all cool with it. Making your bed is pointless; it's only going to get messed up again the next time you sleep in it. You don't see why you can't just have one big cleanup at the end of the week or just before visiting day. Being docked from activities is ineffective, because you would much rather lie around the bunk and do nothing.

LAZY CAMPERS (BUNK MEETING)

3 or 4 Male Campers, 14 years old

Counselor (volunteer):

Every cleanup is a struggle. Nobody participates in cleanup. The floor hasn't been swept; there is an ant problem because of wrappers and food on the floor; the trash is overflowing; wet towels and bathing suits hang from the rafters covered in flies; none of the beds are made; and there are dirty clothes everywhere. First activity is about to blow and it's their favorite activity. Motivate them to clean up.

First Line: "Guys, let's getting going on cleanup. First activity is in five minutes."

240

Male Camper, 15 years old

CAMPER ASKS ADVICE

Counselor (volunteer):

You are a counselor to a division of 15-year-olds. It's nearing the end of the summer, and one of your campers looks very anxious. He asks to talk to you privately about how they will be voting for Color War Captains (a huge honor at your camp). You were a Captain too, so you are happy to help.

Camper (15 years old):

You have had the same camp girlfriend for three summers in a row. Last week you got to second base with her, but she has been pressuring you to go all the way before the end of the summer. You're a virgin and want to find out from you counselor what is the best way to initiate the act and where the most private place to have sex is at camp. You really love your girlfriend and think this is the next step in your relationship. Plus, she says she is the only one of her friends who is still a virgin, and you're afraid that if you don't go all the way with her, she'll decide to lose her virginity with someone else. So no one else becomes suspicious, ask your counselor if you can talk to him privately about "voting for Color War Captains." When you are alone, ask him how old he was when he lost his virginity and about his first time having sex with his girlfriend. Relentlessly pressure him to tell you about how to get to each base. If he refuses, say you'll ask someone else then. If he tries to prevent you, threaten you'll tell about his stash of condoms under a stack of t-shirts on his shelf.

First Line: *"Sorry I lied about Color War voting. I really wanted to ask you how you lost your virginity?"*

CAMPER ASKS ADVICE

Male Camper, 15 years old

Counselor (volunteer):

You are a counselor to a division of 15-year-olds. It's nearing the end of the summer, and one of your campers looks very anxious. He asks to talk to you privately about how they will be voting for Color War Captains (a huge honor at your camp). You were a Captain too, so you are happy to help.

NO RESPECT FOR ELDERS

Male Camper, 15 years old

1st Year Counselor (volunteer):

You're having trouble with a camper who constantly challenges you. He uses bad language and refuses to listen. You walk into the bunk and notice that (yet again) he hasn't gone out to his Elective Period. He can't stay in the bunk unsupervised and you can't stay there with him because you are running another activity. Convince him to go to his Elective.

First Line: "Aren't you supposed to be at basketball?"

Camper (15 years old, 7th summer at camp):

You're an Upper Senior. You're here to have a great summer at camp. Some first-year counselor is on your case about being late to activities. Be rude and disrespectful in how you tell him that it isn't his place to tell you what to do. This is your seventh summer, and this is his only his first. You're not going out to basketball and that's final. (Feel free to mimic him, name call, disrespect him etc.) Counselor speaks first.

NO RESPECT FOR ELDERS

Male Camper, 15 years old

1st Year Counselor (volunteer):

You're having trouble with a camper who constantly challenges you. He uses bad language and re-fuses to listen. You walk into the bunk and notice that (yet again) he hasn't gone out to his Elective Period. He can't stay in the bunk unsupervised and you can't stay there with him because you are running another activity. Convince him to go to his Elective.

First Line: "Aren't you supposed to be at basketball?"

Counselor-Counselor Conflicts

2 Male CITS, 16 years old

GETTING HIGH

Counselor (volunteer):

You notice two CITs (16 years old) sneak off periodically during the day (Free Play, Rest Hour, before or after meals). You think they might be getting high. Confront them.

2 CITs (16 years old):

Both of you have parents who went to camp and who got high while they were there. They've told you this. You've gotten stoned at home and they seem to be cool with it. You brought pot to camp, but have been super careful to hide your stash so no one will find it. In your defense, you are being responsible and only getting high at times during the day when you have no assignments. A counselor suspects what you have been doing. He has no proof, so admit to nothing.

First Line: **"You wanted to see us?"**

GETTING HIGH

2 Male CITS, 16 years old

Counselor (volunteer):

You notice two CITs (16 years old) sneak off periodically during the day (Free Play, Rest Hour, before or after meals). You think they might be getting high. Confront them.

WANDERER

2 Male CITS, 16 years old

Counselor (volunteer):

You notice two CITs sneaking off during free play. You've heard rumors that they have ducked out on other occasions. You circle round and intercept them in the woods. You see hear a lighter being lit. When you enter the clearing you see them holding a lit joint. Challenge them.

First Line: *"What's going on guys?"*

2 CITs (16 years old):

You sneak off to get high in the woods. One of you has already gotten high and is passing the joint to the other when you are discovered by a counselor. Deny that either of you have gotten high yet. Beg the counselor not to tell anyone.

WANDERER

2 Male CITS, 16 years old

Counselor (volunteer):

You notice two CITs sneaking off during free play. You've heard rumors that they have ducked out on other occasions. You circle round and intercept them in the woods. You see hear a lighter being lit. When you enter the clearing you see them holding a lit joint. Challenge them.

First Line: "What's going on guys?"

COUNSELOR IS ALWAYS NAPPING

Male Counselor, 17 years old

Counselor (volunteer):

Your counselors are complaining that one of your Junior Counselors (17 years old) is slacking off, ducking out of assignments, and is taking more than one period a day off. In fact, he naps half the day away. Not surprisingly, he seems to be wide-awake on nights out. They demand that you talk to him. When you walk in the bunk he is sleeping. Assert your authority and motivate him to get back to work.

First Line: "Hey wake up. I think we need to talk."

Counselor (17 years old):

On more than one occasion you've been left to do cleanup by yourself or to take the campers to an unpopular activity. On laundry days, you are the only one making sure that all the laundry bags go out, and the clothes are back on the shelves when the laundry comes back in. You've pulled more than your share of the division's weight for the first half of the summer while everyone else disappeared, kicked back, and relaxed. Now it's your turn to take a couple of extra periods off and enjoy the summer. Your co-counselors have complained to your Group Leader accusing you of being lazy. You are caught sleeping when your Group Leader comes to talk to you.

COUNSELOR IS ALWAYS NAPPING

Male Counselor, 17 years old

Counselor (volunteer):

Your counselors are complaining that one of your Junior Counselors (17 years old) is slacking off, ducking out of assignments, and is taking more than one period a day off. In fact, he naps half the day away. Not surprisingly, he seems to be wide-awake on nights out. They demand that you talk to him. When you walk in the bunk he is sleeping. Assert your authority and motivate him to get back to work.

First Line: *"Hey wake up. I think we need to talk."*

SUSPECTED ABUSE (NON-SEXUAL)

Male Counselor, 18 years old

Counselor (volunteer):

You notice that one of your campers has a big bruise on his arm. You ask him about it, and he proudly says that his favorite counselor gave him some birthday punches. You thank him and after he leaves, ask to meet with the counselor. Visiting Day is just three days away. Talk to the counselor. The Head Counselor covered "birthday punches" and other forms of physical abuse during orientation and know that a counselor can get fired for this.

Counselor (18 years old):

When you were a camper, you loved when your counselors roughhoused with you. Those were some of your fondest memories of camp, because even though they sometimes left bruises (like when you got your birthday punches), it meant that your favorite counselor was having one on one time with you. One of your campers just celebrated his birthday, and you gave him 14 birthday punches. He didn't seem to mind as he has seen his bunkmates giving each other birthday punches on other occasions. But now, another counselor has seen the bruises, and has asked to see you. Visiting Day is just three days away.

First Line: **"You wanted to see me?"**

SUSPECTED ABUSE (NON-SEXUAL)

Male Counselor, 18 years old

Counselor (volunteer):

You notice that one of your campers has a big bruise on his arm. You ask him about it, and he proudly says that his favorite counselor gave him some birthday punches. You thank him and after he leaves, ask to meet with the counselor. Visiting Day is just three days away. Talk to the counselor. The Head Counselor covered "birthday punches" and other forms of physical abuse during orientation and know that a counselor can get fired for this.

COUNSELOR TEASING

Male Counselor, 19 years old

Counselor (volunteer):

One of your campers has complained that one of the counselors in the division has started calling him "Bo." The camper was too upset to tell you what it meant, but now everyone is calling him that and he wants the counselor fired otherwise he's going home. You talk to your co-counselor.

Counselor:

One of your campers has complained that you have given him the nickname Bo, because he smells. (If your co-counselor asks what Bo means, it stands for Body Odor). The nickname has stuck and now everyone is calling him Bo. The camper is very upset and angry. You are frustrated, because you are tired of the struggle to get him to stay clean every day. If you are confronted, deny you did anything wrong or say that the kid is too sensitive. Your counselors teased you and you never got upset. You think this kid needs to toughen up.

First Line: "You wanted to see me?"

COUNSELOR TEASING

Male Counselor, 19 years old

Counselor (volunteer):

One of your campers has complained that one of the counselors in the division has started calling him "Bo." The camper was too upset to tell you what it meant, but now everyone is calling him that and he wants the counselor fired otherwise he's going home. You talk to your co-counselor.

CO-COUNSELOR IS DISRESPECTFUL

Male Counselor, 19 years old

Counselor (volunteer):

You just got wind from one of your campers (8 years old) that your 19-year-old co-counselor has been making fun of you behind your back. He calls you Rick the Stick, because you are a stick in the mud. This is particularly upsetting as you feel you are carrying both his workload in addition to your workload. You have a division of 8-year-olds and you have to do everything for them—clean up, remind them to put on sunscreen, help them sort their laundry…etc. On top of that, you feel that in the bunk you have been the sole "voice of reason" keeping the kids safe, healthy, and happy. He has been acting less like a counselor and more like an unruly camper! Confront him.

Counselor (19 years old):

You are a former camper turned counselor. You requested to be work with older kids, but get stuck with younger kids. Your division of 8-year-olds need help with everything. You are so unhappy that your only entertainment has been making fun of one of your co-counselors, who you have nicknamed him Rick The Stick, because he is so uptight about everything. Your campers laugh hilariously at your jokes, and all of a sudden they really like you. Their encouragement causes you to make more and more jokes about this counselor behind his back. Unfortunately, some blabbermouth has let your little comedy routine leak out, and now your co-counselor wants to talk to you.

First Line: *"What's up?"*

CO-COUNSELOR IS DISRESPECTFUL

Male Counselor, 19 years old

Counselor (volunteer):

You just got wind from one of your campers (8 years old) that your 19-year-old co-counselor has been making fun of you behind your back. He calls you Rick the Stick, because you are a stick in the mud. This is particularly upsetting as you feel you are carrying both his workload in addition to your workload. You have a division of 8-year-olds and you have to do everything for them—clean up, remind them to put on sunscreen, help them sort their laundry…etc. On top of that, you feel that in the bunk you have been the sole "voice of reason" keeping the kids safe, healthy, and happy. He has been acting less like a counselor and more like an unruly camper! Confront him.

COUNSELOR WHO ACTS LIKE A CAMPER

Male Counselor, 19 years old

Counselor (volunteer):

While at an off-campus trip to a roller skating rink, you notice a fellow counselor, Matt, skating really fast and pushing kids down. The skate guard has pulled him aside twice and yet he continues. He has also organized some of the kids to rearrange the letters on one of the signs, making the rink owner more annoyed. The owner pulls you aside and tells you that if that counselor continues to misbehave, he will throw out the whole group and won't allow anyone from your camp to come back again. He insists you talk to him now. He points over to the snack bar where Matt has cut the line and is taking French fries from a camper's order. You pull him aside to talk to him.

First Line: *"Can I talk to you a second."*

Counselor/Matt (19 years old):

Woo-hoo! This is the best skating Social ever. You get your campers to do all the things you did as a camper at roller skating (going super fast, making a line of people and whipping them around the corners, pushing people down, etc.) The skate guards are being their usual uptight selves and have yelled at you numerous times. They've even docked you from skating for 20 minutes. You cut to the front of the snack bar line and grab several French fries from a camper's order when a co-counselor asks to speak to you. The other counselor speaks first.

COUNSELOR WHO ACTS LIKE A CAMPER

Male Counselor, 19 years old

Counselor (volunteer):

While at an off-campus trip to a roller skating rink, you notice a fellow counselor, Matt, skating really fast and pushing kids down. The skate guard has pulled him aside twice and yet he continues. He has also organized some of the kids to rearrange the letters on one of the signs, making the rink owner more annoyed. The owner pulls you aside and tells you that if that counselor continues to misbehave, he will throw out the whole group and won't allow anyone from your camp to come back again. He insists you talk to him now. He points over to the snack bar where Matt has cut the line and is taking French fries from a camper's order. You pull him aside to talk to him.

First Line: **"Can I talk to you a second."**

COUNSELOR ALMOST PEED ON CAMPER'S BED

Male Counselor, 20 years old

Counselor (volunteer):

One of your 11-year-old campers was disturbed by something weird that happened the night before. He woke up to discover his counselor peeing on the floor next to his bed. He tried to say something to the counselor, but he just mumbled and went back to his bed. The camper had trouble falling back asleep, because of the mess on the floor. There were no other witnesses to this event. The camper says that he saw the counselor wiping the floor with a towel after breakfast. You know that this counselor turned 21 years old last night. Find out what happened.

First Line: "So, I heard you had a big night last night."

Counselor (20 years old):

Last night you turned 21 and consequently you had a lot to drink. In the middle of the night you got up to go to the bathroom, but you were so out of it you peed on the floor right next to a camper's bed. He woke up to see you peeing and stumble back to bed. After breakfast, you rush back to the bunk to clean up, but see the camper talking to your Group Leader outside of the cabin. The Group Leader now wants to talk with you. You know you can get fired if it turns out the reason you peed in the wrong place was because you were drunk. So instead, you make up a story about sleepwalking. Because your Group Leader sleeps in another bunk, and because your breath doesn't smell like alcohol, there is no proof. Say whatever you need to in order not to get fired. The other counselor speaks first.

COUNSELOR ALMOST PEED ON CAMPER'S BED

Male Counselor, 20 years old

Counselor (volunteer):

One of your 11-year-old campers was disturbed by something weird that happened the night before. He woke up to discover his counselor peeing on the floor next to his bed. He tried to say something to the counselor, but he just mumbled and went back to his bed. The camper had trouble falling back asleep, because he was afraid the counselor might wake up and do something else. There were no other witnesses to this event. The camper says that he saw the counselor wiping the floor with a towel after breakfast. You know that this counselor turned 21 years old last night. Find out what happened.

First Line: "So, I heard you had a big night last night."

STEALING CANDY 2

Male Counselor, 20 years old

Counselor (volunteer):

You discover from an Upper Hill camper that the culprit stealing your campers' food is actually one of the counselors on your staff. Ask to see him and handle the situation.

Counselor (20 years old):

You and your buddies often snack on your camper's food when they are out at activities. At first it was some Jolly Ranchers or a small bag of potato chips, but it has graduated to Cup o' Noodles. You let the campers believe that older kids are doing the stealing. Everyone borrows each other's socks without asking, so what's the big deal? Besides, by the time 4 PM rolls around you are starving and dinner isn't for another 2 hours.

First Line: "You wanted to see me?"

STEALING CANDY 2

Male Counselor, 20 years old

Counselor (volunteer):

You discover from an Upper Hill camper that the culprit stealing your campers' food is actually one of the counselors on your staff. Ask to see him and handle the situation.

Male Counselor, 21 years old

PORN—PART 2

Counselor (volunteer):

You discover that one of your co-counselors has shown porn to a 13-year-old camper in your division. You ask to speak with him.

Counselor (21 years old):

You had some porn on your iPod and you showed it to a 13-year-old camper in your division so they can learn about the birds and the bees. When you were a camper, you had a counselor who was really cool and did the same thing for you, so what's the big deal?

First Line: "You wanted to see me?"

PORN—PART 2

Male Counselor, 21 years old

Counselor (volunteer):

You discover that one of your co-counselors has shown porn to a 13-year-old camper in your division. You ask to speak with him.

SLEEPWALKING COUNSELOR

Male Counselor, 21 years old

Counselor (volunteer):

One of your 11-year-old campers woke up to discover his counselor getting in bed with him. He tried to stop him, but his counselor just mumbled something and kept trying to lie down. He tells you his breath smelled like mouthwash. Eventually, he succeeded in getting the counselor out of his bed and back to his own bed. The camper had trouble falling back asleep, because he was afraid the counselor might return. You wait until the morning before telling someone. You also know that this counselor turned 21 years old the night before. Address the situation.

Camper (21 years old):

Last night you turned 21 and consequently you had a lot to drink. In the middle of the night you got up to go to the bathroom, but you were so out of it you climbed into the bed next to yours, which had a camper in it. It took the camper around 5 minutes to wake you up enough to get you out of their bed. You flop down into your bed and fall back asleep. After breakfast, you see the camper talking to your Group Leader, who now wants to talk to you. You know you can get fired if it turns out the reason you got into the wrong bed was because you were drunk. Because your breath doesn't smell like alcohol, there is no proof. Say whatever you need to in order not to get fired.

First Line: **"What's up?"**

SLEEPWALKING COUNSELOR

Male Counselor, 21 years old

Counselor (volunteer):

One of your 11-year-old campers woke up to discover his counselor getting in bed with him. He tried to stop him, but his counselor just mumbled something and kept trying to lie down. He tells you his breath smelled like mouthwash. Eventually, he succeeded in getting the counselor out of his bed and back to his own bed. The camper had trouble falling back asleep, because he was afraid the counselor might return. The camper waited until the morning before telling someone. You also know that this counselor turned 21 years old the night before. Address the situation.

DOESN'T WANT TO BE UNPOPULAR   Male Counselor, 24 years old

Counselor (volunteer):

You've noticed that whenever your division of kids needs to be disciplined, your co-counselor never corrects them. And when you decide to admonish them, and ask for him to add anything, he never chimes in. He just stands there with an embarrassed grin and just shrugs his shoulders. Half the time he is the one who started the game of football in the bunk or suggested they do a pile-on on one of the beds. What's worse, is he covers for the kids. You want to know who kicked the door off its hinges, and he lies, and says he doesn't know. At 24 he should be more counselor and less camper. After a bed breaks during the pile-on he initiated, ask to talk to him outside—alone.

Counselor (24 years old):

You are having the summer of your life. You went to camp as a kid, but you were never good at sports or popular. Now that you are 24, you are both. And your kids really love you. They hang out with you during the day, and get crazy with you at night. Last night during OD, you led a raid on the bunk next door and got the other OD really mad. The kids in your group are still laughing about it today! Camp is all about fun, and you are officially their favorite counselor. Problem is, your co-counselor is now getting jealous of your popularity. He is pressuring you to rat out some of your kids. That's his deal, not yours. If he tells you that you need to step up your game and be more of a counselor, tell him you're happy being good cop, while he plays bad cop.

First Line: "Before you freak out, it's just a bed."

DOESN'T WANT TO BE UNPOPULAR

Male Counselor, 24 years old

Counselor (volunteer):

You've noticed that whenever your division of kids needs to be disciplined, your co-counselor never corrects them. And when you decide to admonish them, and ask for him to add anything, he never chimes in. He just stands there with an embarrassed grin and just shrugs his shoulders. Half the time he is the one who started the game of football in the bunk or suggested they do a pile-on on one of the beds. What's worse, is he covers for the kids. You want to know who kicked the door off its hinges, and he lies, and says he doesn't know. At 24 he should be more counselor and less camper. After a bed breaks during the pile-on he initiated, ask to talk to him outside—alone.

COUNSELOR-PARENT
SITUATIONS

SPECIAL TREATMENT—FOOD

Father of 10-year-old Female Camper

Counselor (volunteer):

You are paged to the Main Office to greet the father of one of your 10-year-old campers. His daughter wrote home saying she needed a sleeping bag for her overnight. Since he was in the area, he decided to drop it off in person. As he hands you the shopping bag with the sleeping bag in it you notice it's really heavy. Hidden inside the sleeping bag is a six-pack of soda, several bags of candy, and some Cup-of-Noodles. There is a strict no-food-or-drink policy at your camp. This is the third this parent has tried to sneak food into camp to his daughter. Other parents have tried sneaking food in too, but unsuccessfully. You are confident the bunks are food and drink free. Handle the situation.

Parent:

Your daughter wrote to you saying that she is always hungry in the middle of the day and that she wants you to send her food. She claims that she is the only one that doesn't have food in the bunk, and that other kids' parents have found ways around the no-food-or-drink policy by mailing it inside sneakers or wrapped inside towels. You are an alumnus of this sleep-away camp and your mother used to sneak food to you too. However, both times you tried to sneak in food it was confiscated by the Directors or the Head Counselor. Insist that this food be delivered. If not, demand that everyone else's food is confiscated.

First Line: "Here is the sleeping bag, my daughter wanted."

SPECIAL TREATMENT—FOOD

Father of 10-year-old Female Camper

Counselor (volunteer):

You are paged to the Main Office to greet the father of one of your 10-year-old campers. His daughter wrote home saying she needed a sleeping bag for her overnight. Since he was in the area, he decided to drop it off in person. As he hands you the shopping bag with the sleeping bag in it you notice it's really heavy. Hidden inside the sleeping bag is a six-pack of soda, several bags of candy, and some Cup-of-Noodles. There is a strict no food or drink policy at your camp. This is the third this parent has tried to sneak food into camp to his daughter. Other parents have tried sneaking food in too, but unsuccessfully. You are confident the bunks are food and drink free. Handle the situation.

PARENT CALLS ALL THE TIME   Mother of 11-year-old Female Camper

Counselor (volunteer):

One of your campers is always getting paged for a phone call. Her mother calls every day and gossips for 15 minutes. This has caused several problems. First, she is often gone for all of cleanup and so is never there to do her share of the chores. Secondly, other campers are complaining, because their parents have only called once. And thirdly, because she is gossiping about what's happening in the bunk, the girls are really resenting her and bunk relations are now strained. You've talked to this parent before and told her she can't call anymore, but she lies to the camp office and says she is an aunt or a grandmother. You interrupt this latest call to talk with the mother. Tell her you would like her not to call for at least the next two weeks.

Parent (of 11-year-old Female Camper):

You pay a lot of money to send your daughter away to camp, and you want to make sure that she is safe and happy. You want to know everything that is going on in the bunk so that if your daughter is unhappy about the part she got in the play, or something like that, you can complain to the right people so she gets a bigger part. You are someone who never takes no for an answer, and you can find your way around every rule. If they ban you from phone calls, threaten to take your daughter home.

First Line: *"How dare you take my daughter off the phone. I have a right to talk to her every day!"*

PARENT CALLS ALL THE TIME

Counselor (volunteer):   Mother of 11-year-old Female Camper

One of your campers is always getting paged for a phone call. Her mother calls every day and gossips for 15 minutes. This has caused several problems. First, she is often gone for all of cleanup and so is never there to do her share of the chores. Secondly, other campers are complaining, because their parents have only called once. And thirdly, because she is gossiping about what's happening in the bunk, the girls are really resenting her and bunk relations are now strained. You've talked to this parent before and told her she can't call anymore, but she lies to the camp office and says she is an aunt or a grandmother. You interrupt this latest call to talk with the mother. Tell her you would like her not to call for at least the next two weeks.

BREAKING RULES—BUNK GIFTS

Mother of a 12-year-old Female Camper

Counselor (volunteer):

It is Opening Day of camp and are outside greeting parents. Upon re-entering the bunk you discover that 6 girls are sitting together wearing pink headbands with the camp's logo on it with their backs to three of their bunkmates who don't have headbands and who are reading alone on their beds. After you discover which parent violated the policy about giving out bunk gifts, you ask to speak with her outside.

Parent:

Your daughter had a rough winter. During the school year, some of her bunkmates had parties or sleepovers and she wasn't invited. She felt hurt being left out. This has been going on for a couple of years, but became more pronounced because of all the bat mitzvahs in the division. Your daughter and some of her friends (who didn't fit into any of the other cliques) were often not invited. When she asked you to buy cute headbands for just her friends you didn't see any harm in it. The other girls get to flaunt the t-shirts and sweatshirts they get as gifts for going to these bat mitzvahs, why shouldn't your daughter have something exclusive too.

First line: *"You wanted to speak with me?"*

BREAKING RULES—BUNK GIFTS

Mother of a 12-year-old Female Camper

Counselor (volunteer):

It is opening day of camp and are outside greeting parents. Upon re-entering the bunk you discover that 6 girls are sitting together wearing pink headbands with the camp's logo on it with their backs to three of their bunkmates who don't have headbands and who are reading alone on their beds. After you discover which parent violated the policy about giving out bunk gifts, you ask to speak with her outside.

Parent of a 9-year-old Male Camper

A.D.H.D.

Counselor (volunteer):

You have a camper who is driving you nuts! He has trouble paying attention and focusing on tasks, tends to act without thinking, and has trouble sitting still. He is a good-natured camper, but he is disruptive during activities and some of the other kids are starting to complain. You check his Camper Confidential form, but don't see anything there that would indicate that he has this problem at home, and the Health Center said he is not on any medications. After consulting with the Head Counselor, you decide to call the parents to see if they've noticed similar behavior back home.

Parent:

You are the parent of a 9-year-old boy who was diagnosed 4 years ago with A.D.H.D. (Attention Deficit Hyperactivity Disorder). He has been on medications ever since. The medications actually seem to help calm him and to keep him focused. This is your son's first summer at a sleep away camp. You decided (with the approval of your doctor) to take him off his medications. You do this because you want him to have an amazing time, and you're afraid he'll get teased if his bunkmates see that he is on medication. Also, you live in a small NYC apartment, and you think, maybe what he really needs is to just run around outside to get rid of all that hyper energy. You get a phone call from your son's counselor. Your son has been misbehaving and the counselor is looking for advice. At some point let it slip that he is on meds at home.

First Line: "*Oh Hi! Is everything ok?*"

A.D.H.D.

Parent of a 9-year-old Male Camper

Counselor (volunteer):

You have a camper who is driving you nuts! He has trouble paying attention and focusing on tasks, tends to act without thinking, and has trouble sitting still. He is a good-natured camper, but he is disruptive during activities and some of the other kids are starting to complain. You check his Camper Confidential form, but don't see anything there that would indicate that he has this problem at home, and the Health Center said he is not on any medications. After consulting with the Head Counselor, you decide to call the parents to see if they've noticed similar behavior back home.

[Mime calling on the phone or use phones as props]

CAMPER WANTS TO GO HOME

Counselor (volunteer):

One of your first-year campers (10 years old) is really homesick and wants to go home. He has fun when he is busy and has made some really nice friends, but when he is alone he cries. You feel that he will settle in and overcome his homesickness. Today first-year campers received their first phone calls. He cried during the whole conversation, begging, bargaining, badgering and even threatening them to take him home. Finally, his parents cave and say that if he is not happy by the end of the week, they will pick him up and take him home. As the camper finishes up, you ask to speak to his parents. You think if he stays, he will have an amazing summer. Convince them to change course.

Parent of 10-year-old Male Camper

Parent of 10-year-old Male Camper:

You sent your son to camp, because you wanted him to be less shy, make new friends, and try new things. However, things aren't going as planned and his letters are heartbreaking—begging you to take him home, because he is so unhappy, everyone is mean, the activities suck, the food is lousy, it's rained every day, and he is covered with mosquito bites. Finally, you cave and promise him that if he is still unhappy at the end of the week you will take him home. Your son's counselor wants to try to convince you not to take him home. Stick to your guns until you really get the sense that he is in good hands with this counselor and that keeping him at camp is the best thing for his personal growth.

First Line: *"We promised Matt he could come home next week if he is still unhappy."*

CAMPER WANTS TO GO HOME

Counselor (volunteer):

One of your first-year campers (10 years old) is really homesick and wants to go home. He has fun when he is busy and has made some really nice friends, but when he is alone he cries. You feel that he will settle in and overcome his homesickness. Today first-year campers received their first phone calls. He cried during the whole conversation, begging, bargaining, badgering and even threatening them to take him home. Finally, his parents cave and say that if he is not happy by the end of the week, they will pick him up and take him home. As the camper finishes up, you ask to speak to his parents. You think if he stays, he will have an amazing summer. Convince them to change course.

Parent of 10-year-old Male Camper

Father of a 13-year-old Male Camper

HELICOPTER PARENT

Group Leader (volunteer):

This is the third time a particular parent has called you about his 13-year-old son. Even though you are the boy's Group Leader and know that he is having the time of his life, his father is convinced that his son is miserable. Address the father's concerns.

Parent:

Your 13-year-old son is in his 4th year of sleepaway camp. This year he doesn't seem as enthusiastic about it. His first summer you used to get lots of letters. This summer you received only one. After getting that letter you called the Group Leader to tell him that while the letter was positive, it didn't sound enthusiastic enough. Your second phone call was about a photo you saw on the camp's website. In it your son and his friends briefly interrupted their game of football to pose for a quick picture. Your son is holding a football and is smiling, but there is a small gap between his son and some of his friends, who have their arms around each other—almost like he is detached from the group. And then moments ago, you just spoke to him on the phone and he didn't sound interested in chatting with you or your wife. He kept saying he had to get back to his activity. You are worried there is something wrong with your son, and it's not being addressed. Micromanage the situation.

HELICOPTER PARENT

Father of a 13-year-old Male Camper

Group Leader (volunteer):

This is the third time a particular parent has called you about his 13-year-old son. Even though you are the boy's Group Leader and know that he is having the time of his life, his father is convinced that his son is miserable. Address the father's concerns.

BREAKING RULES—PHONES

Counselor (volunteer):

A parent is on the phone and she is furious with you because you confiscated her son's phone. Prior to the summer all parents receive a handbook and an email reminding them that cell phones are not allowed at camp. This particular camper had two phones: one that he voluntarily turned in the first day of camp, and a second one that his mother told him to keep hidden so he could call home whenever he wanted. Diffuse the situation.

Mother of 15-year-old Male Camper

Parent:

Your 15 year-year-old son likes having his cell phone so he could call home or text his friends. You know there is a rule at camp forbidding cell phones. But one thing you've learned from being a parent, that there is a way around every rule. And if you are persistent and clever enough, you can always get your way. You gave your son two cell phones so that if one gets confiscated he still has a second one to use. Unfortunately, both phones have been confiscated. Your son is unhappy and you are furious. Demand that they return both phones immediately. Threaten to send a third one if his counselor doesn't. If that doesn't work, ask why counselors are allowed cell phones.

First Line: ***"You took my son's phones. I demand you return them to him."***

BREAKING RULES—PHONES

Mother of 15-year-old Male Camper

Counselor (volunteer):

A parent is on the phone and she is furious with you because you confiscated her son's phone. Prior to the summer all parents receive a handbook and an email reminding them that cell phones are not allowed at camp. This particular camper had two phones: one that he voluntarily turned in the first day of camp, and a second one that his mother told him to keep hidden so he could call home whenever he wanted. Diffuse the situation.

Index

D

N

O

P

T

U

V

W

About The Authors

David Fleischner has not missed a summer at camp since birth, joining his parents as a director at Camp Scatico in 1984. He has done extensive volunteer work in camping, serving on the boards of the New York State Camp Directors Association (president), Surprise Lake Camp (president), the American Camp Association's New York Section, and NYCAMP (treasurer). He has written articles on camp counselors and homesickness for The New York Times and Camping Magazine.

John James Hickey has worked as a writer, director, and producer in New York and Los Angeles and internationally in London at The Royal National Theatre. He has spent over 25 summers training staff and teaching film making at Camp Scatico. John is a graduate of the Yale School of Drama, and in his spare time paints portraits, hikes, and plays guitar and piano.

Yvette Silver is a cartoonist, art instructor and caricaturist at special events, where she has drawn over 20,000 humorous portraits. Yvette is the author/illustrator of *Grandparents Run In The Family* and *To Work Is Human, Retirement Is Devine*. She lives in New York City with her husband, Marc, and their two sons, Lance and David.

Made in United States
North Haven, CT
10 May 2022

19068326R00173